I0606093

The Other SIDE

Barzakh and Beyond

OMAR SULEIMAN

The Other Side
Barzakh and Beyond

First published in England by
Kube Publishing Ltd
Markfield Conference Centre
Ratby Lane, Markfield
Leicestershire, LE67 9SY
United Kingdom

Tel: +44 (0) 1530 249230
Website: www.kubepublishing.com
Email: info@kubepublishing.com

Cataloguing-in-Publication Data is available from the British Library.

ISBN 978-1-84774-287-2 Casebound
eISBN 978-1-84774-288-9 Ebook

Proofreading and editing: Wordsmiths
Cover illustration, design and calligraphy: Jannah Haque
Printed by: IMAK Ofset, Turkey.

Transliteration guide

A brief guide to some of the letters and symbols used in the Arabic transliteration in this book.

th	ث	*ḥ*	ح	*dh*	ذ
ṣ	ص	*ḍ*	ض	*ṭ*	ط
ẓ	ظ	ʿ	ع	ʾ	ء
ā	ـَا ـآ	*ī*	ـِي	*ū*	ـُو

May the peace and blessings of Allah be upon him.

Glorified and Majestic (is He).

May Allah be pleased with him.

May Allah be pleased with her.

May Allah be pleased with them both.

May Allah bless them both.

May peace be upon him.

May peace be upon her.

May peace be upon them both.

Contents

A Tribute to Uncle Khaled and His Granddaughter

This book is dedicated to **Uncle Khaled Nabhan** and his 3 year old granddaughter, **Reem,** both of whom are **"the souls of our souls".** They were both tragically killed by the occupation forces during the Gaza genocide, but their souls remain alive in the presence of their Lord.

The following passage is a transcript of uncle Khaled's reflections on how his life dramatically changed after he lost Reem.

كُلَّ يَوْمٍ فِي الصَّبَاحِ، أَذْهَبُ لِزِيَارَتِهِمْ فِي القَبْرِ. كَأَنَّهُمْ نَائِمُونَ، أَتَحَدَّثُ مَعَهُمْ وَأَقُولُ: كَيْفَ حَالُكِ يَا رِيم؟ حَبِيبَتِي. كَانَتْ تَدْعُونِي يَا عَيُوِي. كَيْفَ حَالُكِ؟ كَيْفَ حَالُكَ يَا طَارِق؟ كُنتُ أُرِيدُ أَنْ آخُذَكُمْ فِي نُزْهَةٍ مُمْتِعَةٍ. لَمْ أَسْتَطِعْ فِعْلَ ذَلِكَ. لَمْ أَسْتَطِعْ. كُنتُ أُرِيدُ أَنْ أَشْتَرِي لَهُمْ أَشْيَاءَ بَعْدَ الحَرْبِ. كَانُوا يَسْأَلُونَنِي عَنْ التُّفَّاحِ وَالْبَطِّيخِ وَالْمَوْزِ. لَكِنْ أَيْنَ سَأَجِدُهَا؟ وَعَدْتُهُمْ أَنَّهُ بَعْدَ نِهَايَةِ الحَرْبِ سَنَذْهَبُ إِلَى المَطْعَمِ لِأَكْلِ الكَبَابِ وَالشَّوَارْمَا وَالفَاكِهَةِ، لَكِنَّهُمْ مَاتُوا.

أَهْلُ غَزَّةِ قُلُوبُهُمْ مُمَزَّقَةٌ، كُلُّهُمْ. أَطْفَالُهُمْ حُرِقُوا أَمَامَ أَعْيُنِهِمْ، بَنَاتُهُمْ حُرِقُوا، عَائِلاتُهُمْ حُرِقُوا، عَائِلاتُهُمْ قُصِفَتْ، رِجْلُهُ حُرِقَتْ. قَالَ صَدِيقِي: حَرَقْتُ رِجْلِي بَعْدَ أَنْ لَحِقْتُ بِالْحُجَرِ لِسِتِّ سَاعَاتٍ. وَيَجِبُ عَلَيْكَ أَنْ تَشْكُرَ رَبَّكَ، فَإِنَّكَ خَرَجْتَ بَعْدَ نِصْفِ سَاعَةٍ. أَنَا حَرَقْتُ. كُنتُ تَحْتَ الحُجَرِ وَرِجْلِي تَحْتَرِقُ. النَّارُ كَانَتْ تَسْتَعِرُ وَتَذُوبُهَا، وَلَمْ أَسْتَطِعْ أَنْ أَتَحَرَّكَ. كَانَتِ اللَّيْلَةَ، وَلَمْ يَكُنْ حَوْلِيَ أَحَدٌ. بَعْدَ سِتِّ سَاعَاتٍ، لَمَّا فَاقُوا وَجَاءُوا، فَأَخَذَتْنِي السَّيَّارَةُ النَّاقِلَةُ.

كَمْ كَانَ قَلْبُهُ مُجْتَاحًا بِالْحُزْنِ. لِأَجْلِ أَوْلَادِهِ—تِسْعَةٌ مِّنْهُمْ مَاتُوا. رَجُلٌ آخَرٌ—خَمْسَةَ عَشَرَ طِفْلًا، زَوْجَتُهُ، أَوْلَادُهُ، بَنَاتُهُ، كُلُّهُمْ مَاتُوا. وَاللَّهِ قَبْلَ يَوْمٍ مِنْ مَوْتِهَا، تَخَيَّلْتُهَا تَكْبُرُ وَتَذْهَبُ إِلَى الْجَامِعَةِ وَتَأْتِي إِلَيَّ وَتَقُولُ، يَا سِيدُ أَبُو ضِيَاءٍ—لَكِنَّنِي لَنْ تَقُولَ سِيدُ، سَتَقُولُ يَا عَيُوِي. إِسْمِي عَيُوِي. سَتَقُولُ لِي: نَصِحْنِي فِي تَخَصُّصِي. فِي دَرَجَاتِي. رَبَّنَا يَجْمَعْنِي بِهَا فِي الْجَنَّةِ.

"Every day in the morning, I go and visit them at the grave. It is as if they are sleeping. I converse with them and say: 'How are you, Reem, my love?' She would call me Ya'yu'i. 'How are you? How are you? How are you, Tareq? I wanted to take you all on a fun outing.' I could not do that. I wanted to buy them things after the war.

They used to ask me for bananas, watermelon, and apples. But where am I supposed to get them from? I promised them that after the war was over, we would all go to the restaurant, where I would buy them kabobs, shawarma, and fruit. But they all died.

All the people of Gaza are heartbroken. Everyone's children were burned in front of them: their daughters were burned, their families were burned, their families were bombed, or someone's leg was burned. My friend said, 'I burned my leg after being stuck under the rubble for six hours. And you should thank your Lord, you got out after a half hour. I got burned... I was under the rubble and my leg was burning. The fire was scorching and melting it, and I could not move. It was night time, there was no one around. After six hours, when they woke up and came, the ambulance got me out.'

How heartbroken he must have been. With respect to his children, nine of them died. Another man lost fifteen children; his wife, children, and his daughters all died. I swear a day before she died, I imagined her growing up and going to college and coming to me and saying, 'O Sido Abu Diaa.' But no, she will not say Sido. Instead, she will say Ya'yu'i. My name is Ya'yu'i. She will advise me on my major... and on my grades... May Allah reunite me with her in Paradise."

A few months after this conversation, **Uncle Khaled** was killed as well, and he joined his **granddaughter Reem** in the **Barzakh.** May Allah have mercy on him and all the martyrs of Gaza.

With the permission of Allah ﷻ, we will join them and see them on **the other side**.

Introduction

People sometimes say, "I will see you on the other side." But how certain can one be of this other plane of existence? Where exactly is that "other side", and how can you be sure you will reach it? What is its specific nature and make-up? Can you describe it in a logical and understandable way? Will you be recognised there? Have you seen the permanent home that awaits you? And finally, will you be counted among the righteous or the wicked?

The world around us appears tangible and real, yet there exists another realm at the same time—parallel to this one—unseen to us, though it sees us clearly. Allah ﷻ sees everything, the Angels bear witness to the events of this world and beyond, and the unseen is ever-present. Even the creation surrounding us may perceive that realm more profoundly than we do. And we—each of us—are but one step away from entering it.

Everything begins with a fundamental truth: those whom we have buried from our loved ones are not truly dead. They have merely passed into a special realm known as the Barzakh, a stage of existence between this life and the Hereafter. In that world, the souls of the deceased continue to live: some in peace, others in torment. The souls of martyrs may dwell in the bodies of green birds, flying freely in Paradise, while others may suffer and drown in rivers of blood. Some are reunited with long-deceased loved ones in beautiful homes, while others are subject to terrifying punishment at the hand of the Angels.

What is this realm? Who resides within it? And how does knowledge of this world affect the understanding of our current location? To reflect on the Barzakh is to reflect on our ultimate return to Allah and to reconsider the spiritual path we are on today in a world that is plagued with injustice and confusion.

"...so I may do good in what I left behind." Never! It is only a [useless] appeal they make. And there is a barrier [the Barzakh] behind them until the Day they are resurrected.

AL-MU'MINŪN, 23:100

1

The dead are alive in their graves

Many centuries ago, a soldier trekked in the desert of Kufa, Iraq. His aim was to find the urban centre of the city, but he needed directions from someone familiar with the city's landscape. At last, he crossed paths with someone who was apparently coming from the city. Unbeknownst to the soldier, this individual was one of the most famous scholars and ascetics of the time: Ibrāhīm ibn Adham ﵀. The soldier approached Ibrāhīm ibn Adham and asked him: "Are you a slave?"

Ibrāhīm ibn Adham replied in the affirmative. The soldier then asked Ibrāhīm:

أَيْنَ الْعُمْرَان؟

"Where is al-'umrān (the city dwellings, i.e. the urban area of the city)?"

Ibrāhīm ibn Adham said to the soldier: "Follow me." Shockingly, he led him to a graveyard. The soldier was now confused, and said, "But I asked you to take me to the city dwellings!" Unfazed, Ibrāhīm ibn Adham pointed squarely again to the graveyard and replied, "It is right *here*." Frustrated by what he perceived as mockery, the man struck Ibrāhīm on the head and dragged him into the actual city centre. As they entered, the inhabitants of the city began to gather, alarmed and shocked. They shouted at the soldier: "What are you doing? That is Ibrāhīm ibn Adham!" The man replied, "I asked him if he was a slave," as if that somehow justified his action. They turned to Ibrāhīm ibn Adham and said, "O teacher, why did you not tell him who you were?" He responded, "He asked me if I was a slave, but he did not ask me Whose slave I was. I am a slave of Allah."

They then asked, "What did you do when he struck you?" He replied, "I supplicated for Allah to grant him Paradise." They asked: "Why would you do that?" He replied, "Because I knew I would be rewarded through him, and I did not want him to be punished because of me." The people continued asking, "Then why did you take him to the graveyard in the first place? He was asking for the city dwellings." Ibrāhīm ibn Adham said, "I have noticed that when people move to their graves, they settle there permanently, and none ever return. That, to me, is the true city of settlement."[1]

Ibrāhīm was teaching the people around him a profound truth: while the world may chase what appears to be life, the righteous view the grave as the true abode. Spiritually and practically, they lived in constant readiness for the Hereafter. Imagine if we could walk to the graves of those who came before us and ask them, "What is it like now?" How much would we change if we truly understood the answer?

In a narration reported by Jābir ibn ʿAbdullāh, the Prophet ﷺ described an incident involving a group from Banū Isrā'īl who were once trekking together in a journey. As they passed by a graveyard, they said to one another, "Let us perform two *rakʿahs* (units) of prayer and ask Allah to bring one of the deceased back to life, so that they may inform us about death and the life of the grave." They proceeded to offer two rakʿahs and then made sincere supplication to Allah. In response to their prayer, an Israelite man rose from one of the graves, shaking the dust off from his head. He said, "O people! You asked for nothing except this? I died one hundred years ago, and to this day, the pain and heat of the moment of my death has not yet abated. Can you ask Allah to return me to the state I was in before?"[2]

1 al-Ghazālī, *Iḥyā' ʿUlūm al-Dīn*, vol. 3, 75.

2 Ibn Abī al-Dunyā, *Man ʿĀsha baʿd al-Mawt*, 52.

The fact of the matter is that we do not need the dead to return in order to affirm the reality of death or the certainty of the Barzakh. Every single soul that has ever walked the face of this Earth and passed away is now residing in that unseen realm. Consider this stunning fact: while the current global population approaches 8 billion people, estimates suggest that over 117 billion human beings have lived and died throughout history. All of them—every soul—now exists in the Barzakh.

And since the exact number of the people who lived on this Earth is only known to Allah ﷻ, it is imperative to reflect on His words:

وَقُرُونًا بَيْنَ ذَٰلِكَ كَثِيرًا

"[And We destroyed]...as well as many peoples in between."[3]

Now ask yourself, with full reflection: how long will you live in the Barzakh? The answer is that you will remain in that metaphysical plane of existence until the Day of Judgment. For most of humanity, the duration spent in that realm will far exceed the time on Earth. You could transition into the Barzakh tomorrow and remain there for a thousand years or more. And it is not a state of sleep or a suspension of reality; rather, it is called Ḥayāh al-Barzakh (the Life of the Barzakh) for a reason, as life remains animated in another dimension.

3 *al-Furqān*, 25:38.

In the Barzakh, there is life in every sense of the word: people have families, companions, dwellings, and communities. There is also food, drink, and other forms of sustenance. Even animals exist within that realm. It contains all the features of life, yet functions with a reality that is distinct from this world, characterised with its own laws of time, space, and movement. It is unlike the *dunyā* (temporal world), where people age, and unlike Jannah, where all the inhabitants are of the same age. In the Barzakh, the soul may experience metaphysical realities that transcend what we understand, such as the ability to be in multiple places at the same time, or to traverse distances at incomprehensible speeds.

Reflect on the moment the Prophet ﷺ led all the thousands of Prophets عليهم السلام in prayer at al-Masjid al-Aqṣā, and then—almost instantly—conversed with each of them as he ascended through the seven heavens on the miraculous night of al-Isrā' wa al-Miʿrāj. This means that the same rules of time and space found in this Earth do not apply in the Barzakh. Now imagine this: what if, in the Barzakh, you could be in your grave one moment and beneath the Throne of Allah at the very next second? The more righteous a soul is, the more it gains access to that unseen realm with freedom and dignity, traveling, by Allah's permission, just like one who journeys with 'first class' privileges through the dimensions of this world. And we must be mindful of the fact that the Barzakh is not a hypothetical or future concept: it is actually extant at this very moment. For instance, Mūsā ﵇ and Firʿawn (Pharaoh) are both alive in that realm. The Prophet ﷺ described seeing Mūsā ﵇ standing in his grave, praying.[4] Yet, at this very moment, millions of people continue to recite the Qur'anic verses about his infancy floating alone in the Nile. And while we continue to read of Fir'awn casting believers into ditches of fire as related in the Qur'an, Allah is casting him into a fire of his own in the Barzakh. The Barzakh sets the stage for the Hereafter, where all wrongs and injustices will be addressed by Allah with His unquestionable knowledge.

These are not metaphors or mere symbols. This unseen realm is just as real—if not more so—than the physical world before us. Though we cannot yet see it, we are given glimpses—like temporary pathways—into the Barzakh to remind us of its presence. Sometimes in our sleep, such as through vivid dreams, we cross into it. And when we wake up again, the sight of a grave confronts us as a doorway to an entirely different dimension—one shaped not by fantasy, but by the choices we make in this world. Truly, we are all just one heartbeat away from entering that realm. Imam al-Ḥasan al-Baṣrī ﵀ once addressed the members of this Ummah by saying:

يَا ابْنَ آدَمَ إِنَّمَا أَنْتَ أَيَّامٌ

"O son of Adam! You are nothing but a number of days."[5]

4 *Ṣaḥīḥ Muslim*, 2375.

5 'Abd al-Fattāḥ Abū Ghuddah, *Qīmah al-Zamān 'ind al-'Ulamā'*, 27.

Each passing moment is not just the loss of time; rather, it is the loss of a portion of our very selves. And as for those who wrong us, let us remember that they too are nothing more than a set of days. Their power, their cruelty, and their oppression are all bound by time; all their impressive privileges shall all pass once their appointed time set by their Creator arrives. Allah ﷻ consoled His Prophet ﷺ regarding the oppressive polytheists of Mecca with the following words:

فَلَا تَعْجَلْ عَلَيْهِمْ إِنَّمَا نَعُدُّ لَهُمْ عَدًّا

"So do not be in haste against them, for indeed We are [closely] counting down their days."[6]

In his exegetical comments concerning this verse, the great Companion 'Abdullāh ibn 'Abbās ؓ said:

نَعُدُّ أَنْفَاسَهُمْ فِي الدُّنْيَا

"[Allah intends to say with this verse:] 'We are counting down every single one of their breaths in this life.'"[7]

When you open your eyes in that world, do you truly know which group you will belong to? Will you rise with the *shuhadā'* (martyrs), namely those who gave everything for Allah with infinite sacrifices, such that you will never feel pain again? Or will you be among the oppressors, suffering in the grave as you once made others suffer in this life?

---

6 *Maryam*, 19:84.

7 Ibn Kathīr, *Tafsīr Ibn Kathīr*, vol. 9, 295.

Will you be counted among the sincere believers, resting in peace, surrounded by light, awaiting a joy even greater than what they now feel? Or will you be among the disbelievers and hypocrites, already tasting the punishment they were warned about? Or finally, will you find yourself at in intermediate point that lies in between? You might actually be a believer that is flawed, inconsistent, and registering both good and bad deeds, waiting to see if your sins will catch up with you or hoping that Allah will cover them with His mercy. The Barzakh is the decisive moment of time where everything is made clear and a person's path is determined. There are no more masks and no more distractions in this plane; only the truth prevails. That is why when ʿUthmān ibn ʿAffān ﵁ stood beside a grave, he would weep until his beard was soaked with his tears. And when asked, "You do not cry like this when Paradise and Hell are mentioned, so why here?" he replied by relaying that the Prophet ﷺ said:

إِنَّ القَبْرَ أَوَّلُ مَنَازِلِ الآخِرَةِ، فَإِنْ نَجَا مِنْهُ فَمَا بَعْدَهُ أَيْسَرُ، وَإِنْ لَمْ يَنْجُ مِنْهُ فَمَا بَعْدَهُ أَشَدُّ مِنْهُ

"Indeed, the grave is the first station of the Hereafter. If this stop is easy, what comes after will be easier. But if it is hard, then what follows will only be harder."[8]

But the grave does not have to be a place of fear of the unknown. For the believer, it can be a place of peace, comfort, and reward. It can be the first true portion of rest after a life of striving, hardship, and faith for the righteous soul.

---

8 *Sunan Ibn Mājah*, 4267.

For some, the grave is not a prison, but rather it is a source of liberation for the soul. The great Successor Masrūq ibn al-Ajdaʿ ﵀ said:

مَا مِنْ بَيْتٍ خَيْرٌ لِلْمُؤْمِنِ مِنْ لَحْدٍ، قَدِ اسْتَرَاحَ مِنْ هُمُومِ الدُّنْيَا، وَأَمِنَ مِنْ عَذَابِ اللَّهِ

"There is no home better for a believer than his grave. For he has been relieved from the affairs of this world and granted security from the punishment of Allah."[9]

And for those of us who have lost someone who brought light and joy to our lives, the grave is not just a place of parting; it can also be the place of reunion. It can be a place where, by the mercy of Allah, we are once again united with those we loved so dearly in this world. ʿUthmān ibn Sawdah ﵀ once narrated that his mother, Rāhibah, a righteous woman, looked at him before her death and said, "My son, do not forsake me, neither in life nor in death." After her passing, he would visit her grave just as he used to visit her home, making *duʿā'* (supplication) for her with devotion and love. One night, he saw her in a dream: she was radiant, beautiful, surrounded by silken garments and the incense of Paradise. She turned to him in his vision and said, "I rejoice when you visit me. So do not stop visiting me."[10]

At this moment, turn your attention to your own predestined grave, the one that is already written for you, and the one you will soon visit and eventually reside in for an unknown

9 Ibn Abī Shaybah, *al-Muṣannaf*, vol. 7, 148.

10 Ibn al-Jawzī, *Ṣifah al-Ṣafwah*, vol. 2, 253.

length of time. What does that grave look like? What does it feel like? And what does it smell like? When 'Abdullāh ibn Ghālib ﷺ passed away, a beautiful and fragrant scent rose from his grave after he was buried. Later, someone saw him in a dream and asked about that fragrance. He replied, "That was the breath of my recitation and my thirst."[11] His recitation of the Qur'an and his thirst during fasting had left behind a fragrance that filled his grave.

Before the next Ramadan commences, reflect deeply about what you are building spiritually with your fasts, your prayers, your recitation of the Qur'an, and your *du'ā'*. Your grave is already under construction. With every righteous deed, it breathes a little easier. It becomes more welcoming, more fragrant, and more spacious. It is not just a resting place; rather, it is the entrance to a reality far more enduring than this fleeting world. So ask yourself now: What does your other side look like? What have you prepared for the fateful moment when you cross that threshold? And what will you find there that finally makes sense of the pain, the confusion, and the trials of this life?

11 Ibn Rajab, *Lata'if al-Ma'arif*, p. 300

2

They are watching your world

If you are an avid viewer of sports, you have likely heard an announcer shout several times in the middle of a game, "He shoots, he scores!" You have also likely seen a stadium packed with thousands of fans, all watching a game with intense focus. Every movement on the field, every decision, and every last-second shot draws out a reaction: cheers, gasps, and chants. And when a spectacular moment unfolds, the crowd erupts in celebration, perhaps even chanting a single name, that is, the name of the most valuable player. For many, that kind of attention is the ultimate dream. Whether it is shooting imaginary game-winning shots alone in an empty gym, daydreaming of wealth and fame, or watching the likes and comments pile up on an Instagram post, so much of our behaviour is driven by the desire to be seen and to be validated. People often say: "I want to be seen, I want to be heard, and I want to be felt." This is a recurring theme in therapy, in our relationships, and in our daily struggles. Such cravings are dangerous and have led to a myriad of psychological and spiritual diseases, as they cause humans to turn away from their ultimate purpose decreed by their Creator ﷻ.

You already have an audience that is greater than any crowd in a stadium, larger than any following on social media, and more significant than any panel of critics. You are constantly being observed. Above you, around you, beneath you, and beyond your senses, the entire unseen world is aware of you. You may not perceive their attention, but your soul is not insulated from their presence and watchful gaze; in other words, your soul is actually always on stage, and is observed by millions of Angels.

The only reason for why you cannot hear the commentary of your spectators is that you cannot see your audience. You live in the limitations of the *dunyā* (temporal world), and Allah, in His wisdom, has veiled much of the unseen realm from human perception. But the worldly creation around you sees and hears in ways you cannot imagine. An eagle sees with a sense of clarity that is eight times greater than ours: it can spot a rabbit from three kilometres away. Bees perceive ultraviolet patterns on flowers that we cannot even detect. Cats see in near-total darkness. And yet, it is you—the human being—who is the central subject of the unseen world's gaze. The Prophet ﷺ said: "When you hear the crowing of a rooster, ask Allah for His favour, for it has seen an Angel. And when you hear the braying of a donkey, seek refuge in Allah, for it has seen a *shayṭān* (devil)."[12] In another narration, he ﷺ told us that all the creatures hear the punishment of the grave except for us. Allah has spared us that auditory horror out of His infinite mercy. Reflect upon that point for just one moment: if just hearing the cries of the dying through our screens is so difficult today, what would happen if we could hear the cries of the dead—our own loved ones—in their graves? We would be shocked and paralyzed, unable to carry on with life.

This mercy from Allah ﷻ is not limited to the plane of the Barzakh alone. Imagine if your vision was enhanced such that it could see the microscopic world, such as particles floating every time someone sneezes or dust mites crawling on surfaces like insects. Would you be able to sit in comfort among others if such entities could be observed? The answer is a resounding no. Through His knowledge and mercy, Allah has given us exactly what we need in the right measure so that we may fulfill our purpose: to know Him. Our senses are not flawed; quite to the contrary, they are perfectly designed for our test. We are not

12 *Ṣaḥīḥ al-Bukhārī*, 3303.

He is with you by His knowledge, at every moment of your life. So when you reflect on the audience surrounding your stage, do not forget the most important One watching at all times: Allah.

meant to see everything. In contrast, we are meant to believe in what is known as the *ghayb* (unseen) through the signs He has shown us. It is for this reason that the Prophet ﷺ said:

أُوصِيكَ أَنْ تَسْتَحِيَ مِنَ اللَّهِ تَعَالَى كَمَا تَسْتَحِي مِنَ الرَّجُلِ الصَّالِحِ مِنْ قَوْمِكَ

"I advise you to be shy of Allah just like how you would from a righteous person from your people."[13]

Naturally, you can see people with your eyes, and you know they see you. As a person, you intuitively know very well how differently you would act if a righteous person were constantly with you, inspecting every move, recording you with a camera, or even just being physically present beside you. You would be more careful with your words, more mindful of your actions, and more conscious of how you appear. But Allah ﷻ—Who is greater than any righteous human being—sees you all the time. His presence is not limited by proximity or perception; He is with you by His knowledge, at every moment of your life. So when you reflect on the audience surrounding your stage, do not forget the most important One watching at all times: Allah. Every other observer—whether Angel, jinn, or human—only matters if their gaze brings you closer to Him.

Always be mindful of this fact: your life is not a performance for the world. In actual fact, it is a presentation of your soul to your Creator ﷻ. And what is on display is not your appearance, your wealth, or your talents. Rather, it is your

13 al-Ṭabarānī, *al-Muʿjam al-Kabīr*, 7738.

heart, your intentions, and what your soul spiritually inclines toward. Among those observing your deeds and thoughts are Angels. They see you, support you, and pray for you. Their encouragement is not applause; rather, it is *du'ā'* (supplication). They ask Allah to forgive you when you repent, raise your rank when you perform righteous deeds, and protect you when you are vulnerable or falling into wrongful conduct. You might even have a devoted Angel in your corner, encouraging you in a way that you cannot hear, but nevertheless their call reaches the heavens. But there are also *shayāṭīn* (devils) from the jinn in the unseen world, whispering, plotting, and even conversing around you in ways you cannot perceive. Regarding the watchful conduct of Shayṭān and his evil associates, Allah states:

إِنَّهُ يَرَاكُمْ هُوَ وَقَبِيلُهُ مِنْ حَيْثُ لَا تَرَوْنَهُمْ

"Surely he and his soldiers watch you from where you cannot see them."[14]

But those devils are not just whispering from the outside; they can flow through your bodily cavities and even move within you, depending on how much space you apportion them. The more room your heart offers, the more influence they have. This is not a passive struggle. Rather, it is a relentless and daily battle for your soul. And if you do not take control, you will be overwhelmed by the evil forces around you. That is why you have to train your heart to dispel the whispers of the Shayṭān (Devil) and submit to the guidance of Allah ﷻ.

14 *al-A'rāf*, 7:27.

The more you seek Him, the more clarity you gain. The volume of Shayṭān begins to fade, and you start to feel the quiet and steady nudges of the Angels that encourage and call you toward what is right.

Just imagine reaching the level of ʿUmar ibn al-Khaṭṭāb ﷺ, who was described as *muḥaddath* (the one spoken to and inspired by Allah). He was a man so in tune with divine guidance that it was as though the Angels spoke to him and guided his words and actions. Most people, by contrast, live as *mutawaswas* (the one constantly afflicted by the whispers of Shayṭān). But here is something to reflect on: just as your social media feed changes based on what you watch, like, and follow, your soul develops its own algorithm. If you keep seeking Allah, your heart will begin to see and hear differently. Your spiritual perception sharpens and your horizons will change and become aligned with your higher moral purpose as a servant of Allah. But if you keep feeding your desires, your vision becomes clouded, and the whispers only grow louder.

As your soul turns toward Allah ﷻ, it is not just the Angels who support you. The entire creation responds in a positive fashion. From the great beasts of the land to the smallest insects, from the birds in the sky to the fish in the sea, all of them will begin to pray for you. The world around you, seen and unseen, becomes your ally. In other words, when you live in accordance with a worldview that is based on the pursuit of Allah's pleasure, everything in existence starts pleading for your success. Yet, as Allah notes, we are unaware of their words of glorification:

وَإِن مِّن شَيْءٍ إِلَّا يُسَبِّحُ بِحَمْدِهِ وَلَٰكِن لَّا تَفْقَهُونَ تَسْبِيحَهُمْ

"There is not a single thing that does not glorify His praises—but you cannot comprehend their glorification."[15]

In stark contrast, you also cannot see how a single sin, even one you merely intend, can cause everything from Angels to insects to turn away from you. That does not mean that every animal that avoids you is reacting to your sin, but it reminds us that our souls are already being engaged by the unseen world. Just like in the case of the Barzakh, where the soul is fully visible, in this life too there are hidden realities responding to your soul, not your appearance. Your soul, in fact, has a scent that it emits to other beings of this world. Sufyān al-Thawrī ﷺ was asked how the Angels detect someone's intention. He said, "When a person intends to do good, the Angels perceive the smell of musk coming out of him. Whereas if he intends to do evil, they smell this wretched odour coming out of him."[16]

The Earth itself prays for the believer. As Allah states:

فَمَا بَكَتْ عَلَيْهِمُ ٱلسَّمَآءُ وَٱلْأَرْضُ

"Neither heaven nor earth wept over them, nor was their fate delayed."[17]

---

15 *al-Isrā'*, 17:44.

16 Ibn Taymiyyah, *Majmu al-Fatawa* 4:253

17 *al-Dukhān*, 44:29.

Ibn ʿAbbās ﷺ commented on this verse by stating: "For the believer, the heavens and the Earth weep because of the good influences they would leave behind." He also said:

تَبْكِي ٱلْأَرْضُ عَلَى ٱلْمُؤْمِنِ أَرْبَعِينَ صَبَاحًا

"The Earth would weep over a believer for 40 days."[18]

The Prophet ﷺ once described the stench of an evil soul at death so vividly that he covered his own nose with a cloth, showing how unbearable its foul odour would be. In contrast, the fragrance of a righteous soul draws even the attention of the Angels in the heavens. They ask, "Where is this beautiful scent coming from?" This is undoubtedly a sign of a soul beloved to Allah.

There is also no doubt that the Angels bear witness to the oppression on Earth. When Ibrāhīm ﷺ was thrown into the fire, they waited anxiously for permission to help him. Even the frogs, as related in some reports, tried to carry drops of water in their mouths to put out the flames. But Allah had already decreed something better for His beloved Prophet ﷺ, as He issued the following directive: "O fire! Be cool and safe for Ibrāhīm!"[19]

To the Angels, we are not merely numbers. This point is poignantly expressed in a powerful narration concerning Imam

18 *Tafsir at-Tabari, Tafsir Ibn Kathir*

19 *al-Anbiyā'*, 21:69.

Aḥmad ibn Ḥanbal ﵀ during his trial and torture, an ordeal that is known as the Miḥnah. A man once said, "I witnessed Imam Aḥmad enduring the lashes with patience and strength, despite his physical weakness. I wept because of it. That very night, I saw in a dream as if a voice called out to me, saying, 'If only you could see the Angels in the sky boasting about him while he was being beaten.' I asked, 'Did the Angels know of Aḥmad's suffering?' The voice replied, 'There was not a single Angel in the heavens except that it had witnessed his ordeal.'"[20] Building off this beautiful report, we may ask: how many Angels witnessed the burning of the young 19-year-old *ḥāfiẓ* (memoriser) of the Qur'an, Shaban al-Dalou, in the current genocide in Gaza? The Angels are thus aware of our pain and pray for our success in this world and the Hereafter.

Besides the Angels, other entities are aware of our state and actions as well, such as our deceased loved ones who are in the Barzakh. Ṣadaqah ibn Sulaymān al-Jaʿfarī ﵀ said, "After the death of my father, I committed a sin that I later deeply regretted. I then saw my father in a dream, and he said to me, 'My son, we were once extremely delighted by your deeds, thinking them those of the righteous. But I was deeply ashamed of you on one occasion. So do not disgrace me again in front of the other believing souls.'" Ṣadaqah's neighbour then related, "From that day onward, Ṣadaqah would weep and call upon Allah every night in his *qiyām* (voluntary night prayers), saying: "O Rectifier of the righteous, O Guide of the misguided, and

20 Abdul Ghani al-Maqdisi, *al-Mihna 'ala Imam Ahlis Sunnah*, 18

O Merciful to the sinners, grant me a beautiful return to You such that I never return back to what caused me shame."[21]

In a beautiful narration reported by Anas ﷺ, the Prophet ﷺ is reported to have said:

إِنَّ أَعْمَالَكُمْ تُعْرَضُ عَلَى أَقَارِبِكُمْ وَعَشَائِرِكُمْ مِنَ الْأَمْوَاتِ، فَإِنْ كَانَ خَيْرًا اسْتَبْشَرُوا بِهِ، وَإِنْ كَانَ غَيْرَ ذَلِكَ، قَالُوا: اللَّهُمَّ لَا تُمِتْهُمْ، حَتَّى تَهْدِيَهُمْ كَمَا هَدَيْتَنَا

"Your deeds are presented to your close relatives who have passed away. If they are good, they celebrate. And if they are not good, they say: 'O Allah, do not cause them to die until You have guided them just as You had guided us.'"[22]

It is reported that 'Abbād ibn 'Abbād once visited Ibrāhīm ibn Ṣāliḥ ﷺ while he presided over Palestine as its governor. Ibrāhīm asked him for sincere counsel. 'Abbād replied, "Your deeds are shown to those who have passed, and among them is the Messenger of Allah." Upon hearing this, Ibrāhīm wept until his beard was soaked. Imagine the moment Ibrāhīm returned to the unseen. It is likely that he met the Prophet and heard what had been said about him.

Entering the Barzakh is like going behind the scenes and having a direct gaze at the processes backstage, facing those who have been silently watching all along. But do not wait for death to confront that reality. Reflect now: Who are you

21 Ibn Abi Dunya, *al-Manamat*, 17

22 *Musnad Aḥmad*, 12683.

in the eyes of those who witness your life from beyond this world? How would the Prophet ﷺ view your choices today? Are the Angels proud of you, or have the devils claimed their hold? What reports have reached your loved ones who have already entered the grave and are in the Barzakh?

Reflect on this question carefully and prepare for a solid answer for it, starting from this very moment: what will your legacy be in a realm you have not yet reached?

"...so I may do good in what I left behind." Never! It is only a [useless] appeal they make. And there is a barrier [the Barzakh] behind them until the Day they are resurrected.

AL-MU'MINŪN, 23:100

3

They may have another name for you

What is the name you are known by here, and what do they call you on the other side? A significant portion of our lives is spent towards building a positive name and reputation for ourselves in this world. From early on, there is a deep desire to be recognised, to be remembered, and to have our names spoken with admiration by others. Even in psychology, it is said that a person's name is among the strongest triggers for attention and emotion. People internally glow up when their name is mentioned by someone they admire, and particularly when it appears on a screen, a certificate, or a plaque. But have you ever asked yourself what your name is with Allah ﷻ? Is it possible that you carry a different name in the unseen realm than the one people use in this worthless plane known as the *dunyā* (temporal world)? The purpose of this chapter is to explore these themes and questions.

There is a beautiful Hadith of the Prophet ﷺ which touches on the theme of names. In it, the Prophet ﷺ made the following *du'ā'* (supplication), giving us valuable insights about the Names of Allah:

أسألُكَ بِكُلِّ اسْمٍ هُوَ لَكَ سَمَّيْتَ بِهِ نَفْسَكَ أَوْ أَنْزَلْتَهُ فِي كِتَابِكَ أَوْ عَلَّمْتَهُ أَحَدًا
مِنْ خَلْقِكَ أَوْ اسْتَأْثَرْتَ بِهِ فِي عِلْمِ الْغَيْبِ عِنْدَكَ

"I ask You [O Allah] by every name that You have named Yourself, or every name that You have revealed in Your Book, or every name that You have taught to any one of Your creations, or every name that You have kept unto Yourself in the knowledge of the unseen that is with You alone."[23]

From this report, we can infer that there are special Names of Allah that are known only to certain members of His creation, Names that perhaps the Angels call upon, though we have never heard of them. And there are Names that remain entirely hidden in the unseen realm, known only to Him Himself. We know Him as al-Raḥmān (the Possessor of Mercy), al-Raḥīm (the Bestower of Mercy), and by many other beautiful Names. But we can only imagine how many

23 *Musnad Aḥmad*, 3712.

Have you ever asked yourself what your name is with Allah ﷻ? Is it possible that you carry a different name in the unseen realm than the one people use in this *dunyā*?

more exist, specifically majestic Names that have never been revealed to mankind, and Names that He has used in ways we cannot yet comprehend.

Our own beloved Prophet ﷺ also had many names. In one narration, he ﷺ states:

إِنَّ لِي أَسْمَاءً: أَنَا مُحَمَّدٌ، وَأَنَا أَحْمَدُ، وَأَنَا المَاحِي الَّذِي يَمْحُو اللهُ بِي الكُفْرَ، وَأَنَا الحَاشِرُ
الَّذِي يُحْشَرُ النَّاسُ عَلَى قَدَمِي، وَأَنَا العَاقِبُ ، وَالعَاقِبُ الَّذِي لَيْسَ بَعْدَهُ نَبِيٌّ

"I have several names. I am Muhammad. I am Aḥmad. I am al-Māḥī, the one through whom Allah erases disbelief. I am al-Ḥāshir, the one at whose feet the people will be gathered on the Day of Judgement. And I am al-ʿĀqib, the one after whom there is no Prophet."[24]

Moreover, the Prophet ﷺ added in another Hadith:

وَنَبِيُّ التَّوْبَةِ وَنَبِيُّ الرَّحْمَةِ

"And [I am] the Prophet of repentance, as well as the Prophet of mercy."[25]

Some of these names were bestowed directly upon the Prophet ﷺ by Allah, such as Muhammad and Aḥmad. Others, like al-Ṣādiq (the Truthful) and al-Amīn (the Trustworthy), were titles that he earned through the nobility of his character and the beauty of his dealings throughout his blessed life. These names were not merely labels; rather, they were reflections

24 *Ṣaḥīḥ al-Bukhārī*, 4896.

25 *Ṣaḥīḥ Muslim*, 2355.

of who he was as a person, with these qualities being recognised by both friend and foe. In a parallel fashion, Allah describes Prophet Yaḥyā ﷵ, the son of Zakariyyā ﷵ, with a similar honour. He says:

يَا زَكَرِيَّا إِنَّا نُبَشِّرُكَ بِغُلَامٍ اسْمُهُ يَحْيَىٰ لَمْ نَجْعَل لَّهُ مِن قَبْلُ سَمِيًّا

"[The Angels announced:] 'O Zakariyyā! Indeed, We give you the good news of a son, whose name will be Yaḥyā, a name We have not given to anyone before.'"[26]

This was a glad tiding not only of how the character of Yaḥyā ﷵ was marked by *ḥayā'* (modesty), but also a subtle indication of his martyrdom. The name Yaḥyā itself means "he lives" (third person imperfect verb), and the *shuhadā'* (martyrs) are described by Allah as *aḥyā'* (alive), though we do not perceive their lively state in the metaphysical plane of existence.

But are such positive manifestations also found in the names of believers who are not from the Prophets? The answer is a resounding yes. In a notable Hadith, the Prophet ﷺ said:

مَا مِنْ عَبْدٍ إِلَّا لَهُ صِيتٌ فِي السَّمَاءِ فَإِذَا كَانَ صِيتُهُ فِي السَّمَاءِ حَسَنًا
وُضِعَ فِي الأَرْضِ وَإِذَا كَانَ صِيتُهُ فِي السَّمَاءِ سَيِّئًا وُضِعَ فِي الأَرْضِ

"There is not a servant of Allah except that they have a reputation in the heavens. If they have a good reputation in the heavens, it descends to those on Earth. And if they have a bad one in the heavens, it also descends to those on Earth."[27]

---

26 *Maryam*, 19:7.

27 al-Ṭabarānī, *al-Mu'jam al-Awsaṭ*, 5248.

But what will your name be in the heavens? What will you be known for in the sight of Allah and His Angels? Unbeknownst to you, this is a choice that you are writing every day. The first implication of this Hadith is reputation, namely how one is spoken of in the unseen realm. It is not only the name given to you by your parents that matters. Perhaps there is a name that your deeds are writing for you, one that reflects your true nature before your Creator. There is a beautiful story about 'Umar ibn 'Abd al-'Azīz that offers some golden insights into this matter. He once said: "One night, I saw the Prophet ﷺ in a dream. He was standing in a green meadow and said to me, 'You will be entrusted with the affairs of my Ummah. When that time comes, do not shed the blood of the people.' Then ﷺ he said:

فَإِنَّ اسْمَكَ فِي النَّاسِ عُمَرُ، وَاسْمَكَ عِنْدَ اللَّهِ جَابِرٌ

'For your name among the people is 'Umar, but your name with Allah is Jābir (the Mender and Comforter).'"[28]

This was not just a name, but also a divine recognition of his role, earned through character and destined by purpose. 'Umar ibn 'Abd al-'Azīz was not just following the footsteps of his grandfather 'Umar ibn al-Khaṭṭāb by assuming his same name, but he tried to reach his level through his good deeds and piety. His God-consciousness is what led him to be bestowed with yet another name and title: Jābir. So ask yourself: What name are your actions writing for you in

28 Ibn al-Jawzī, *Sīrah 'Umar ibn 'Abd al-'Azīz*, 249.

the unseen? You can carve another name for yourself in the unseen, but you must earn it through virtue and goodness.

As for the name given to you by your parents, it holds no weight unless it is upheld by your actions. A noble name is not enough without noble character; a name is only as honourable as the person who carries it. How many people today bear the name Muhammad, yet live in direct contrast to the one they were named after? A person may be called ʿAbdullāh (lit. Servant of Allah), but in reality they are known by their attachment to this world, just as the Prophet ﷺ described some people as really being ʿAbd al-Dīnār or ʿAbd al-Dirham, namely the slave of gold and silver coins respectively. History also offers powerful examples of this sobering fact. A tyrant once caused devastation in Medina. Though his name was Muslim ibn ʿUqbah, the people called him Mujrim (the Criminal). And Abū al-Ḥakam (the Father of Wisdom) was renamed by the Prophet as Abū Jahl (the Father of Ignorance) due to his arrogance, disbelief, and opposition to the call of Islam.

On the other hand, consider the case of Abū Bakr al-Ṣiddīq رضي الله عنه. Due to his virtuous conduct as an earlier believer, he earned the title al-Ṣiddīq (the Paragon of the Truth) because of his unwavering belief and loyalty to Islam. It was not a title that was given lightly. Rather, it was a title that he attained through sincerity, steadfastness, and immediate affirmation of the truth, especially at the most critical moments. But such a name is not inherited; it is earned. One must trek the path of *ṣidq* (truthfulness) in order to be granted that honour in the sight of Allah. For as the Prophet ﷺ said:

وَيَتَحَرَّى الصِّدْقَ حَتَّى يُكْتَبَ عِنْدَ اللهِ صِدِّيقًا

"[A person] continues to manifest the truth until he is written with Allah as a ṣiddīq."[29]

Consider how many years a person spends striving for titles like PhD, MD, or any other academic or professional distinction. These titles require dedication, consistency, and sacrifice. Likewise, earning a name or title in the heavens—one that carries weight with the Angels and is honoured by Allah—requires both sincere and sustained effort. And how beautiful it is to have your name mentioned often in the heavens and praised by those who dwell there! This is why the Prophet ﷺ encouraged abundant remembrance of Allah. He said that among the best forms of remembrance are *tasbīḥ* (glorification of Allah), *tahlīl* (proclaiming the oneness of Allah), and *taḥmīd* (praising Allah). These words—when sincerely uttered—rise up and encircle the Throne of Allah, buzzing like bees, carrying with them the names of those who said them. How could anyone not love to be remembered in this way? The golden rule is this: the more you remember Allah by His beautiful Names, the more He mentions you by names of honour, that is, names shaped by

29 *Ṣaḥīḥ Muslim*, 2607.

your deeds, purified by your sincerity, and beautified by your remembrance. For as He states:

فَاذْكُرُونِيٓ أَذْكُرْكُمْ

"Remember Me; I will remember you."[30]

If you remember Allah in private, He remembers you to Himself. And if you remember Him in a gathering, He remembers you in a gathering far greater: the gathering of the Highest Companions, who are an elite class of Angels. When Allah mentions your name with praise in the heavens, it no longer matters how often your name is spoken with hate on Earth. The polytheists attempted to mock the Prophet by calling him Mudhammam (the Dispraised), but he was, and will always be, Muhammad (The One Who is Praised). His name remained elevated, regardless of their slander. And just as there is envy on Earth, there is envy in the heavens. Iblīs grew jealous of Prophet Ayyūb ﷺ because his name was mentioned repeatedly in the highest ranks of the heavens due to his unwavering righteousness on Earth.

But this honour is not reserved only for the Prophets or the well-known servants of Allah. Any sincere believer—no matter how hidden from the world—can have their name remembered in the highest company. As one famous Arabic proverb puts it, the yardstick of a person's standing is their *taqwā* (God-consciousness), not their worldly fame or standing:

30 *al-Baqarah*, 2:152.

كَمْ مِنْ مَشْهُورٍ فِي الْأَرْضِ مَجْهُولٍ فِي السَّمَاءِ؟ وَكَمْ مِنْ مَجْهُولٍ
فِي الْأَرْضِ مَعْرُوفٍ فِي السَّمَاءِ؟

"How many famous people on Earth are unknown in the heavens? And how many unknown people on Earth are celebrated in the heavens?"

But what if no one speaks about you here? What if you are a "nobody" in the eyes of this world? Know that it means little to be unknown on Earth as long as you are known in the heavens. During the reign of 'Umar ibn al-Khaṭṭāb ﷺ, a man returned from battle and listed the names of the martyrs, adding: "Then there are other people whom Amīr al-Mu'minīn (the Leader of the Believers) does not know." 'Umar wept and replied, "And what does it matter if 'Umar does not know them, as long as Allah knows them?"[31] Taking this story as an analytical starting point, ask yourself: What is your name in the heavens? How often is it mentioned in that unseen realm? Perhaps your name is Fārūq (the One Who Distinguishes Between Truth and Falsehood) because you are standing firm in an age of confusion, lies, and deception. Perhaps you are known as 'Ādil (the Just) because you are upholding fairness in a world dominated by oppression. Or maybe your name is Ṭāhirah (the Pure One) because you guard your heart and soul from the stains of immodesty and corruption.

What do the records in the Barzakh say about you? What are the headlines that carry your name in that realm? It is not

31 Ibn Kathir, *al-Bidayah Wa al-Nihayah*, 10:124

impossible to find the answer to this question. Reflect on the qualities described in the Qur'an—both praiseworthy and blameworthy—and ask: Which of these best descriptions and labels best describe me? And beyond that internal reflection, you can truly identify how you are known in the heavens by analysing how you live right now. It was said to the Prophet ﷺ: "What is your view of a person who does good acts, and the people praise him for those virtuous acts?" The Prophet ﷺ replied:

تِلْكَ عَاجِلُ بُشْرَى الْمُؤْمِنِ

"That is the early glad tiding for the believer."[32]

Then comes the day of your *janāzah* (funeral), when the witnesses on the Earth testify to who you truly were. If today were the day of your funeral, and people stood to speak about you, what is the one quality they would all agree upon, and that is genuinely true of you? This is a momentous question, because the Prophet ﷺ said to the ones who witnessed the funeral procession and burial:

أَنْتُمْ شُهَدَاءُ اللَّهِ فِي الْأَرْضِ

"You are the witnesses of Allah on Earth."[33]

After your soul departs and enters the Barzakh, it hears these testimonies for itself. At that moment, you are no longer called by your given name alone. You are called by the names that Allah has known you by and the names the Angels were

---

32 *Sunan Ibn Mājah*, 4225.

33 *Ṣaḥīḥ Muslim*, 949.

informed of, all of which are based on your deeds and your character. The Prophet ﷺ described how, when the righteous soul ascends, it does not pass by a group of Angels except that they ask:

مَا هَٰذِهِ الرُّوحُ الطَّيِّبَةُ؟

"What is this pure and sweet-smelling soul?"[34]

And the Angel carrying it responds: "This is so-and-so, the child of so-and-so," calling the soul by its most beloved names that reflect its true nature. But in stark contrast, when the soul is wicked, the Angels will say:

مَا هَٰذِهِ الرُّوحُ الْخَبِيثَةُ؟

"What is this foul, filthy soul?"[35]

And it too will be called by the names it earned, harsh and humiliating titles that reflect its reality before Allah. Thus, it is imperative to ask who you really are. When you were born, your soul was assigned a reality. Your spiritual record did not say male or female when it was activated, but *saʿīd* (blessed) or *shaqī* (wretched). And when you die, your soul carries another label, *ṭayyibah* (pure) or *khabīthah* (corrupt), based on what you amassed during your time on Earth. And that name—*qua* spiritual identity—is what matters most at that moment. It is not the name that is etched on your tombstone, but the one written on your reservation for what lies beyond it that matters.

---

34 al-Bayhaqī, *Shuʿab al-Īmān*, 390.

35 al-Bayhaqī, *Shuʿab al-Īmān*, 390.

4

What do my dreams really mean?

What are you dreaming about these days? Are there deeper messages and meanings in the dreams that you witness from time to time? Have they come to warn you, guide you, or have they left you in a state of confusion? What do your dreams reveal about who you truly are? Are they simply a mirror reflecting what has preoccupied your thoughts by day, or do they comprise a message from the unseen, namely a whisper from a world beyond this one? When you dream of your deceased loved ones, is it they who visit you, or is it your soul that crosses into their realm for a moment?

Dreams can serve as a window into the depths of your own soul, or as a doorway into the next life that patiently awaits you. Every night, your soul departs your body and journeys to its next station, only to be returned by the mercy of Allah ﷻ, giving you yet another opportunity to seek forgiveness, return to the right path, and to make amends before a night comes when it does not return to the world anymore.

There was a 28-year-old young man in Gaza named ʿĀmir, who was an in-house patient in Nasser Hospital. A video shows his face marred by brutal injuries. Not only did he lose an eye, but his body was further battered by multiple surgeries. Despite this fate, ʿĀmir accepted his fate with tranquillity and contentedness. His doctor was visibly moved with this sight, and asked him during an interview, "What is going on with you? How can you be so joyful, even after enduring such brutal injuries?" ʿĀmir responds with calm certainty: "Look, I am 28 years old, and I have been in this hospital for 40 days. But those [i.e. the moment he was injured] were the best five seconds of my entire life." In order to explain this paradoxical statement, ʿĀmir shared his background story in further detail:

جَاءَنِي شَخْصٌ فِي الْمَنَامِ، فِي مَكَانٍ لَا أُرِيدُ وَصْفَهُ، لِأَنَّ الطَّاوِلَةَ هُنَاكَ رُبَّمَا كَانَتْ أَجْمَلَ مِنْ أَيِّ شَيْءٍ فِي الْعَالَمِ. ٱلشَّوْكَةُ ٱلَّتِي ٱسْتَخْدَمَهَا لِيَقْطَعَ لِي، عِنْدَمَا قَالَ لِي: «أُرِيدُ أَنْ أُطْعِمَكَ بِيَدِي»، كَانَتْ أَجْمَلَ مِنْ أَيِّ شَيْءٍ فِي الْعَالَمِ. أَطْعَمَنِي زَعْتَرًا، وَبِمُجَرَّدِ أَنْ وَضَعَهُ عَلَى شَفَتَيَّ، ذَابَ. لِمُدَّةِ أَرْبَعِينَ يَوْمًا، لَمْ آكُلْ شَيْئًا، وَلَمْ أَرْغَبْ فِي أَيِّ شَيْءٍ آخَرَ بَعْدَ ذَلِكَ بِسَبَبِ حَلَاوَةِ طَعْمِهِ. وَكَانَتْ رُؤْيَا، حُلْمًا رَأَيْتُهُ. ثُمَّ جَاءَنِي شَخْصٌ وَقَالَ: «قُمْ وَصَلِّ صَلَاةَ

الغَائِبِ لِصَدِيقِكَ.» أَمْسَكَ بِكَتِفِي هَكَذَا. فِي ٱلْيَوْمِ ٱلتَّالِي، ٱسْتُشْهِدَ صَدِيقِي، وَمَعَهُ ثَلَاثُونَ فَرْدًا مِنْ عَائِلَتِهِ. يَا اللّٰهُ! أَيْنَ؟ فِي خَانْ يُونُسَ.

"A person came to me in a dream, in a place I struggle to describe, because even the table in that vision was more beautiful than anything I have ever seen in this world. The fork he used, as he said to me, 'I want to feed you with my own hands,' shimmered with a beauty beyond anything earthly. He then fed me za'atar man'oushe. *And the moment it touched my lips, it melted; it was so tender and so sweet that I have never tasted anything like it. For forty days, I had not eaten. But after that moment, I did not desire food anymore. That taste was so real and so otherworldly that it satisfied something far deeper than hunger. It was a vision and a dream that stayed with me. Then someone appeared before me and said, 'Get up and pray* ṣalāh al-ghā'ib *(absentee funeral prayer) for your friend.' He placed his hand firmly on my shoulder. The very next day, news came that my friend had been martyred, along with thirty members of his family. [All of this happened in] Khan Yunis."*

This story sharply parallels and brings to mind an incident from the time of the Prophet ﷺ. The latter account speaks of the profound connection between dreams, the unseen, and the world of the soul. Anas ibn Mālik ﵁ narrated that the Prophet ﷺ loved good dreams. Each morning, he would ask his Companions, "Who among you saw a good dream last night?" And if a person was known to be upright in character, the Prophet would give greater attention to what they saw, recognising that sincerity in the heart often reflects truth in vision. One day, a woman came to the Prophet ﷺ and said, "O Messenger of Allah, I saw myself entering Jannah." She went on to describe a powerful scene: she saw twelve men, all of them covered in blood, who were already in Paradise. Then, she saw Allah ﷻ say to a group of Angels:

اِذْهَبُوا بِهِمْ إِلَى نَهَرِ الْبَرْزَخِ

"Take them to the River of Barzakh."

So the Angels took them to that river. And when the martyrs emerged, she described them in the following terms:

وَوُجُوهُهُمْ كَالْقَمَرِ

"Their faces were shining like the full Moon."

They were then seated on golden chairs, surrounded by plates of fresh food and dates. The female Companion then said, "I sat with them and ate with them." And just as she finished describing this vision to the Prophet ﷺ, a man came rushing in with news: those very twelve men—whom the Prophet ﷺ had earlier sent on an expedition—had just been martyred.[36] So what was this dream? Were they truly in Jannah already? Was this the realm of Barzakh? In reality, this dream reflected a real encounter between souls and the realm of the unseen.

36 Ibn Rajab al-Ḥanbalī, *Ahwāl al-Qubūr wa Aḥwāl Ahlihā ilā al-Nushūr*, 342.

The dreams of the righteous often reflect the purity of their hearts. In Islam, there is some space for recognising the significance of dreams, particularly true dreams, as a form of inspiration or early glad tidings.

In the field of psychology, dreams are often described as "the royal road into the unconscious". They reveal to us what lies beneath the surface level, namely what occupies our inner world, what truly concerns us, and where our hearts are most deeply connected. In Islam, we also recognise that dreams are replete with inner spiritual meanings. The dreams of the righteous often reflect the purity of their hearts. You will find that their dreams are frequently filled with the Prophet ﷺ along with visions of Jannah, or with glad tidings for others who are righteous. Why is this the case? This is because their hearts, minds, and souls are already immersed in those realities while awake, so they see them again while asleep. And your dreams, too, mirror what spiritually fills you. Thus, our dreams can be meaningful, even those that arise from within ourselves. In Islam, there is some space for recognising the significance of dreams, particularly true dreams (which are known as *ru'yā ṣāliḥah*), as a form of inspiration or early glad tidings. However, we are also cautioned not to inflate their value to the point of escapism. In other words, we do not live by what we see in our dreams while ignoring the clear guidance of the Qur'an and the Sunnah. The Prophet ﷺ did not nurture a sleeping Ummah that sought guidance through dreams. He was the man whose eyes would sleep but whose heart never did. His heart remained awake, always being connected to Allah. When the heart is truly awake—even while the eyes are closed—extraordinary things can happen.

After all, the Prophet ﷺ said:

أَصْدَقُكُمْ حَدِيثًا، أَصْدَقُكُمْ رُؤْيَا

"The most truthful of you in speech are those with the truest dreams."[37]

A *ṣiddīq* (paragon of the truth) is one whose dreams are marked by true guidance, precisely because their hearts are grounded in truthfulness. It is for this reason that the Prophet ﷺ warned that one of the gravest forms of falsehood is to fabricate a dream. Lying about a dream, he said, is among the most serious kinds of lying in the sight of Allah.[38] As the Day of Judgment draws nearer and the world becomes increasingly deceptive—such that truth is often disguised as falsehood, and vice versa—Allah grants believers true dreams as a form of divine consolation and guidance. The Prophet ﷺ said that in such confusing times the believer's dream will almost always materialise and manifest in the world. As he said: "In the end of times, the dreams of a believer will hardly ever fail to come true."[39]

The truth value embedded in dreams has always held a high place in our tradition. In fact, the Prophet ﷺ described true dreams as being "one forty-sixth of prophethood".[40] Now, one may ask how that proportion is understood in such exact terms. From the 23 years during which revelation was sent to the Prophet ﷺ, the first six months consisted

37 *Ṣaḥīḥ Muslim*, 2263.

38 *Ṣaḥīḥ al-Bukhārī*, 3509.

39 *Ṣaḥīḥ al-Bukhārī*, 7017.

40 *Ṣaḥīḥ al-Bukhārī*, 6983.

solely of true dreams before any verbal revelation began. Six months is one-half of a year, and one year is 1/23rd of 23 years. Therefore, six months equals 1/46th of the total period of revelation. However, the distinction remains clear: while dreams were a portion of revelation for the Prophet ﷺ, they do not confer prophethood upon others. Unlike the Prophets ﷺ, whose dreams are always true, the dreams of ordinary people can be a mixture of truth, falsehood, and the workings of the subconscious.

The Prophet ﷺ taught us that there are three types of dreams. First, there is the category of *ru'yā ṣāliḥah*: a true and righteous vision that is from Allah. Then, there is *ru'yā taḥzīn min al-shayṭān*, a distressing or disturbing dream which comes from Shayṭān with the intent to cause fear, sadness, or confusion. Finally, there is *ḥadīth al-nafs*, that is, dreams that stem from the soul's internal dialogue; they are essentially a reflection of one's thoughts, worries, and daily experiences. The Prophet noted that this third type is the most common. He instructed that if a person sees something in a dream that they dislike, they should neither seek its interpretation nor speak of it. Instead, he said, they should stand up and pray, and seek the protection of Allah.[41] In doing so, they prevent any harm from descending upon them.

In another narration, the Prophet ﷺ offered a powerful metaphor. He said that the interpretation of a bad dream is like a bird tied by its leg, hovering in the air. If a person

41 *Ṣaḥīḥ Muslim*, 2263.

assigns it an interpretation and animates it, they risk having that meaning "fall" and apply to them.[42] In other words, a harmful dream may not come to pass unless one pursues its meaning and thereby anchors it to reality. So, the prophetic instruction is clear: do not pursue or share disturbing dreams, but rather, seek refuge in Allah and move on by exercising trust in His protection.

Despite the categorization of dreams, the truth remains that they can serve as a window into the unseen. A dream may contain divine inspiration conveyed through the Angels, or even offer a glimpse into future events. Sometimes dreams include encounters with the souls of the deceased, bringing solace to the living. The Prophet ﷺ once heard a Companion narrate a dream involving him, and he remarked, "Indeed, the souls meet."[43] This statement raises profound questions. Is this type of meeting literal or symbolic? Do the souls of the living travel to the realm of the dead during sleep, or do the souls of the deceased visit the realm of the living? While the precise mechanism remains within the knowledge of Allah, these narrations affirm that our dreams may involve real encounters in the unseen world, especially for those whose hearts remain spiritually attuned.

Without any doubt, Allah has the power to connect souls across dimensions, even while they remain physically in this

---

42 *Sunan Abī Dāwūd*, 5020.

43 *Musnad Aḥmad*, 21864.

world. One of the most striking examples of this is found in the incident involving ʿUmar ibn al-Khaṭṭāb ﷺ. As he once delivered a *khuṭbah* (sermon) in Medina, he suddenly called out three times, in rapid succession:

يَا سَارِيَةُ الجَبَلَ

"O Sāriyah, the mountain!"[44]

He was addressing Sāriyah ibn Zunaym ﷺ, one of his commanders. At that very moment, Sāriyah was stationed thousands of miles away in Persia, facing a surprise ambush from behind a mountain. Miraculously, Sāriyah heard the voice of ʿUmar and responded by repositioning his troops, an act that turned the tide of the battle and led to their success. Ibn al-Qayyim ﷺ, reflecting on such events, affirmed: "The souls of the living can indeed meet and interact in ways known only to Allah, whether they are awake or asleep."[45] This interaction is not limited to the material realm of the dunyā (temporal world). Just as souls may connect across physical distances in this life, Allah will most certainly permit the souls to meet across dimensions, especially in the next realm of the Barzakh. And every night, we are given a glimpse into that unseen realm; for as the Prophet ﷺ taught, sleep is a minor form of death, and each night our souls are lifted and returned by the decree of Allah. These moments—often unnoticed—are part of the continuous journey of the soul,

44 al-Muttaqī al-Hindī, *Kanz al-ʿUmmāl fī Sunan al-Aqwāl wa al-Afʿāl*, 35783.

45 Ibn al-Qayyim, *al-Ruh*, 1:92

with encounters, messages, and meanings that transcend the boundaries of the physical world. For as Allah Himself states:

اللَّهُ يَتَوَفَّى الْأَنفُسَ حِينَ مَوْتِهَا وَالَّتِي لَمْ تَمُتْ فِي مَنَامِهَا

"Allah calls back the souls [of people] upon their death as well as [the souls] of the living during their sleep."[46]

During times of sleep, the soul departs the body, yet remains tethered to it. This attachment allows life to continue, though the level of consciousness reaches its lowest state. The deeper the level of sleep, the greater that the soul's connection to this world fades, and the more it potentially slips into the realm of Barzakh. Conversely, in shallow sleep, the mind remains close to wakefulness, making it more likely for dreams to consist of *ḥadīth al-nafs*—the replaying of thoughts and emotions—rather than visions from the unseen. Ibn al-Qayyim ﵀ explains in *Kitāb al-Rūḥ* that during actual death, the soul exits from the mouth, as the Prophet ﷺ described, and the eyes follow it as it departs. One may even witness this phenomenon occur in the face of the *shahīd*, whose eyes open and mouth smiles upward, as if witnessing their soul's ascension. However, during sleep, the soul exits only partially—like a ray—through the nostrils, while remaining attached to the body. Ibn al-Qayyim ﵀ adds that a truthful soul may ascend to the heavens and return, whereas a lying soul may encounter the *shayāṭīn* (devils), leading to corrupted visions; this distinction is key. Ibn 'Abbās ﵄ remarked that the souls of the living and the dead meet during dreams, inquiring one another about important events.

46 *al-Zumar*, 39:42.

Allah then withholds the souls of the deceased and returns the souls of the living to their bodies, as mentioned in the Qur'an.

But how can one discern the nature of a dream? If a dream is truly from Allah, it will bear one of the following signs: 1) It commands good or forbids evil, for this is the consistent message of Allah to His servants; 2) it materialises and comes true, for the speech of Allah is always truth, 3) it increases you in *īmān* (faith), as Allah sends what nourishes the faith of the believer.

Among all dreams, none is greater than a vision of the Prophet ﷺ, which is certainly from Allah, for Shayṭān cannot imitate his noble form. Such a vision is a divine honour and glad tiding for the one who sees it. To meet him in a dream is no ordinary occurrence; it is a rare and sacred gift from Allah. For Shayṭān cannot impersonate him; thus, seeing the Prophet in your dream is a sign of divine favour and connection.

But if a dream originates from Shayṭān, consider what his intentions are. In short, Shayṭān aims to instil fear, stir the base desires, encourage sin, or present dreams that contradict revelation, even if they appear pleasant or profound. Thus, any dream that seems to deliver a "new sign" or "revelation" outside of what has already been firmly established in the *dīn* (religion) is not from Allah. If the dream is merely *ḥadīth al-nafs*, then it is psychological in nature. It may relate to unresolved tensions or fleeting memories. You may see things that seem noble—such as the *masjid*, the Qur'an, or other acts of worship—intermingled with nonsensical or unrelated images. These dreams reflect the contents of the heart and mind at rest, not messages from the unseen.

As for true dreams and meetings between souls, they are gifts from Allah ﷻ. Neither the living nor the dead have the power to initiate or control these encounters. If a deceased loved one appears in someone else's dream but not in yours, know that it is Allah alone Who decides which souls meet during sleep and which messages are conveyed. In such visions, you may see a righteous soul radiant and joyful, dressed beautifully, and smiling in serenity, all of which likely constitute signs of their peace. Other times, you may see them distressed, indicating an outstanding need, such as an unsettled debt, a requested prayer, or an undone deed. One striking example is that of Thābit ibn Qays رضي الله عنه, a martyr in the Battle of Yamāmah. After his death, he appeared in a dream to a Companion and informed him of a shield he had lost, naming its exact location. He also requested that Abū Bakr رضي الله عنه use the shield's worth to repay a debt. The shield was found just where he described, and Abū Bakr acted upon the deceased's wishes. In other cases, the dream may impart a word of advice. After the passing of Imam Sufyān al-Thawrī رحمه الله, his students would see him in their dreams, continuing to benefit from his wisdom. One of them, Sufyān ibn 'Uyaynah رحمه الله, said, "I saw my teacher in a dream and said to him, 'Give me advice.' He responded, 'Maintain the company of fewer people.'"[47] Others saw him in

47 Abu Nu'aym al-Isfahani, *Hilyat al-Awliya*, 6:386

The deeper the level of sleep, the greater that the soul's connection to this world fades, and the more it potentially slips into the realm of Barzakh.

Jannah, and when asked how he attained such a rank, they received answers that were consistent with his character in life. Ibn al-Jawzī ﷺ narrates that someone once saw Sufyān al-Thawrī in a dream and asked him, "What did Allah do with you?" He replied, "The moment I was placed in my grave, it felt as though I was immediately brought before the Lord of the worlds. Then someone called out to me, 'O Sufyān!' I responded, 'Yes.' He asked, 'Do you recall a moment in your life when you chose Allah over your own desires?' I said, 'Yes.' And right after that, grand platters of food from Paradise were brought before me."[48] Another man, Suʿayd ibn al-Khims ﷺ, shared a dream where he saw Sufyān al-Thawrī flying from one palm tree to another, reciting the following verse continuously:

الْحَمْدُ لِلَّهِ الَّذِي صَدَقَنَا وَعْدَهُ

"Praise be to Allah Who has fulfilled His promise to us."[49]

How heartwarming it is to witness a deceased loved one—a parent, a teacher, or a friend—tasting the sweetness of Jannah in a dream. Sometimes you may even see them happily anticipating your arrival, telling you your time is near. These are all possible glimpses, but it is essential to remember that you do not live through your dreams; rather, you live through your decisions. Your choices while awake determine your true

48 Ibn al-Jawzi, *Sifat as-Safwa*, 2:87

49 *al-Zumar*, 39:74.

destination in the Afterlife. It is also crucial that people do not turn bad dreams into modes of self-fulfilling despair, nor treat good dreams as a measure of piety. As we sleep, our eyes may close, but our hearts must remain awake, steadfast in faith and commitment.

"...so I may do good in what I left behind." Never! It is only a [useless] appeal they make. And there is a barrier [the Barzakh] behind them until the Day they are resurrected.

AL-MU'MINŪN, 23:100

5

How to see the Prophet ﷺ in a dream

You can actually meet the Prophet ﷺ tonight, but only if you choose to live like him today. Imagine feeling his warmth. Picture standing in his presence, and seeing the light of his smile. Envisage your loved ones—those who emulated him and lived like him—now sitting with him. It is likely that they are all waiting for you to correct your vices and mistakes, so that you can join them in the Eternal Garden.

The story of the woman in Gaza who dreamt of the genocide before it happened demonstrates the power of dreams and how our blessed Prophet ﷺ is aware of the current state of his Ummah. News of her vision spread across phones and groups, just before the very images of destruction began to fill those same screens. In her account, she said: "I saw the Prophet sitting in the courtyard of al-Masjid al-Aqṣā. And people were coming to him from every corner of the earth." But these were not just any people. For as she noted: "They were the oppressed Muslims. I saw Muslims from Syria, from Yemen, from Iraq, from the Uyghurs, from Kashmir, and from Somalia." All of them were oppressed, wounded, and silenced, yet they rapidly gathered around their Prophet ﷺ. And as the crowd swelled around him, he ﷺ smiled and said:

لَتَدْخُلُنَّ الْجَنَّةَ زُمَرًا

"You will enter Paradise in great multitudes."

Then he ﷺ said to them:

نَصْرُ اللهِ آتٍ فَأَبْشِرُوا

"The victory of Allah is coming, so receive glad tidings."

Immediately after this, someone cried out:

يَا رَسُولَ اللَّهِ، وَمَتَىٰ هَذَا الْفَوْزُ؟

"O Messenger of Allah, when will this victory come?"

The Messenger of Allah ﷺ replied:

الشَّهَادَةُ هِيَ الْفَوْزُ

"Martyrdom is the true victory."

Then, the Prophet ﷺ began to recount his own trials, which included the following events: 1) the Meccan years, 2) the persecution and boycott, 3) the Hijrah, 4) the Battle of Uḥud, and 5) the long nights of pain and fear. All of this was recounted in a way to indicate that he had gone through this difficult path as well. The sister witnessing the dream then said that a great army appeared; they were so vast in number, and their bodies were so magnificent that they shone like the full Moon. The Prophet ﷺ pointed to them and declared:

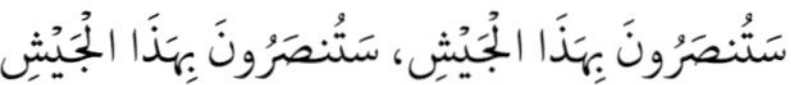

"You will be given victory through this army. You will be given victory through this army."

They charged forward, fighting on behalf of the Muslims until they attained victory. At the final moments of the dream, the woman turned to the Prophet ﷺ and asked:

أَأَنْتَ رَسُولُ اللَّهِ؟

"Are you really the Messenger of Allah?"

In reply, he ﷺ said:

أَنَا نَبِيُّكُمْ مُحَمَّدٌ، أَنَا نَبِيُّكُمْ مُحَمَّدٌ

"I am your Prophet Muhammad. I am your Prophet Muhammad."

These dreams are priceless gifts. They have carried the Ummah through generations of darkness. They have revived hearts, guided nations, and sustained individuals at their lowest points. Anas ibn Mālik ﷺ once said: "I served the Prophet ﷺ for ten years in Medina, and I never saw anyone more beautiful or more blessed than him. He was the best of creation and the finest in character."[50] Anas lived with the Prophet ﷺ in this world, but after the Prophet ﷺ passed away, Anas lived on for nearly 90 years. He thus spent many decades without enjoying the opportunity to see the blessed face of the Prophet ﷺ. Imagine the depth of his longing, where he would miss the Prophet every single day. Al-Muthannā ibn Saʿīd ﷺ narrated that Anas ﷺ said:

وَاللهِ، مَا مِنْ لَيْلَةٍ إِلَّا وَأَنَا أَرَىٰ فِيهَا حَبِيبِي صَلَّى اللهُ عَلَيْهِ وَسَلَّمَ

"By Allah, not a night passes except that I see my beloved in it."[51]

Anas began to weep when he said this. After all, he served the Prophet ﷺ for ten years. Then, for ninety years, he saw him

50 *Ṣaḥīḥ al-Bukhārī*, 2820.

51 *Musnad Aḥmad*, 13267.

every night in his dreams. And by the permission of Allah, he is now with him once again. When Anas passed away—at an age exceeding 100 years—he requested to be buried with what remained in his possession from the Prophet, such as his hair and his walking stick. Imagine that reunion in the Barzakh after nearly a century of yearning. But the greatest blessing from Allah is that you do not need to have lived with the Prophet to be connected to him.

How does a person become honoured by seeing the Prophet ﷺ in a dream? It begins with sincere love expressed through actions and constant *ṣalawāt* (salutations). The Prophet ﷺ said: "No one sends a *salām* (greeting) upon me except that Allah returns my soul to me so I may return the *salām* to him."[52] And in another narration, he said: "Among the best of your days is Friday. So send *ṣalawāt* upon me frequently, for your *ṣalawāt* are presented to me." The Companions asked, "O Messenger of Allah, how will our *ṣalawāt* be displayed to you when your body has mixed with the earth?" He replied:

إِنَّ اللّٰهَ حَرَّمَ عَلَى الْأَرْضِ أَجْسَادَ الْأَنْبِيَاءِ

"Allah has barred the earth from consuming the bodies of the Prophets."[53]

This means that at this very moment, if you send *salām* upon the blessed Prophet, his soul responds to you from a perfect body that is untouched by time. He also said to Muʿādh ibn

52 *Sunan Abī Dāwūd*, 2041.

53 *Sunan Abī Dāwūd*, 1047.

Jabal ؓ: "The people closest to me are the people of piety, whoever they are, and wherever they may be." But one should bear in mind that seeing him in a dream is not the measure of righteousness. Living by his Sunnah is the true yardstick one should abide by. Some of the most righteous members of the Ummah never saw him in their dreams; inversely, those who are distant from Allah may be shown the Prophet ﷺ not as a mark of status, but as a means of guidance. Still, there is no doubt that whoever sees him has truly seen him. So live like him, love him deeply, and send abundant *ṣalawāt* upon him. And perhaps then by Allah's facilitation you will see that noble face in your dream.

The Prophet ﷺ said: "Whoever sees me in a dream has truly seen me, for Shayṭān cannot assume my form."[54] This Hadith imparts two essential points: 1) Shayṭān cannot imitate the Prophet, 2) in order for it to be truly the Prophet ﷺ, he must appear in his actual and known form that is delineated in the *shamā'il* literature, which outlines the features of the Prophet ﷺ. In addition, it is important to note that the way in which a person sees the Prophet ﷺ in a dream can carry different meanings. Imam Ibn Ḥajar ؒ reports from Ibn Abī Jamrah ؒ the following: "If one sees the Prophet ﷺ in a beautiful state, it is a sign of soundness in the dreamer's religion. But if the Prophet ﷺ appears wounded or harmed, it reflects a deficiency in the dreamer's own practice of religion."[55] One man came to Ibn Sīrīn ؒ and said, "I saw myself burying the Prophet ﷺ with

54 *Ṣaḥīḥ al-Bukhārī*, 6997.

55 Ibn Hajar al-Asqalani, *Fath al-Bari*, 12:387

my own hands." Ibn Sīrīn interpreted this as a grave matter; he said it signified that the person was engaging in *bid'ah* (religious innovation) in Islamic practices, as if he was burying the Sunnah.[56] Conversely, some scholars reported dreams of themselves digging up the grave of the Prophet ﷺ. Among them was Imam Abū Ḥanīfah, who dreamt that he was unearthing the grave of the Prophet ﷺ and sorting through his blessed bones.[57] The dream was interpreted to mean that he would devote himself to sorting through the narrations of the Prophet ﷺ, which is undoubtedly an honourable task. Nūr al-Dīn Zengī, the great leader who preceded Ṣalāḥ al-Dīn, once saw the Prophet ﷺ in a dream looking distressed. The Prophet ﷺ pointed to two men and said, "Save me from these two dogs."[58] Alarmed by this vision, Nūr al-Dīn sent two trusted soldiers to Medina with a detailed description of the men. They were found exactly as described: they were two undercover Crusaders. In a blatant act of desecration, they had been digging a tunnel in an attempt to reach the grave of the Prophet. By the blessing of the dream, their plot was thwarted. Imam al-Bukhārī once dreamt that he was fanning flies away from the face of the Prophet. This was interpreted as his role in sifting the corpus of prophetic traditions and removing the fabricated Hadiths falsely attributed to the Messenger.

56 Al-Dhahabi, *Siyar 'Alam an-Nubala*, 4:617

57 Ibn al-Mulaqqin, *Ḥadā'iq al-Awliyā'*, vol. 1, 32.

58 'Abd al-Raḥmān ibn Qāsim, *al-Durar al-Saniyyah fī al-Ajwibah al-Najdiyyah*, vol. 5, 399.

During the time of Imam Aḥmad ibn Ḥanbal ﵀, while he was being persecuted and tortured, he saw the Prophet ﷺ in his dreams comforting him, saying, "Be patient, O Aḥmad." Others around him also saw dreams affirming his righteous path. Imam al-Shāfiʿī ﵀ narrated a dream in which the Prophet ﷺ said to him: "O Ibn Idrīs, give glad tidings to this young man Aḥmad. He will be tested in the religion of Allah. He will be called to speak falsehood but will refuse. He will be beaten with the whip. But in any case, Allah will spread through him knowledge that will remain until the Day of Judgment."[59] An elderly man once came forward and said: "I saw the Prophet in a dream, along with Abū Bakr and ʿUmar ﵄, crossing the canal of Baghdād. The cloak of the Prophet slipped from his right shoulder. You, O Aḥmad, rushed forward and placed the cloak back on his shoulder. The Prophet turned to you, as did Abū Bakr and ʿUmar ﵄, with them all saying: 'Rejoice, for you are our companion tomorrow in Jannah.'" The man then said to those around Imam Aḥmad: "The cloak that Aḥmad put back on the shoulder of the Messenger was the Sunnah, for Aḥmad has been chosen by Allah to restore it to the people."

It is important to add here that seeing the Prophet ﷺ in a dream is not a random occurrence. Oftentimes, it mirrors how he would have visited you in this world by affirming your righteousness, advising you toward a better path, or comforting you in times of hardship. That prophetic gift continues to this

---

59 Jamīl al-Shāṭṭī, *Mukhtaṣar Ṭabaqāt al-Ḥanābilah*, p. 12.

day. Take the example of Dr. Aafia Siddiqui, who is perhaps the most wronged woman of our time. She once shared that in the midst of her suffering, when the Ummah had all but forgotten her, she saw the Prophet in a dream; he was consoling her in her painful state of solitary confinement. Many others in their darkest hours are also granted this most precious gift. One of the most beautiful accounts is from Shaykh ʿAbd al-Ḥamīd Kishk. On the morning of Friday, 6 December 1996, he turned to his son and asked, "How old was the Prophet when he passed away?" His son replied, "You already know that, the answer is 63." Shaykh Kishk smiled and said, "*Alḥamdulillāh* (All praise is due to Allah), I am 63." He went on to describe a dream he just had the night before. He saw the Prophet ﷺ, along with Abū Bakr and ʿUmar, all of whom had passed away at the age of 63. The Prophet looked at him and said:

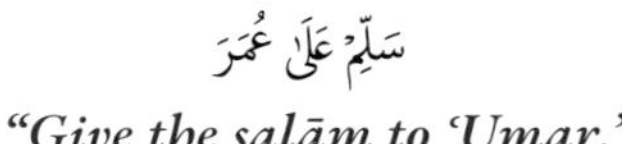

"Give the salām to ʿUmar."

So he gave *salām*, and then in the dream, he saw himself dying. He described a scene where the Prophet ﷺ, Abū Bakr, and ʿUmar were washing his body. It so happened that on that very same day—which happened to be the day of Jumuʿah—Shaykh Kishk died in his *sujūd* (prostration), just as he had long prayed to Allah for. But that was after a life filled with love for the Prophet, and a sincere effort to carry his light forward in the world. Ibn al-Qayyim said that true love for the Prophet ﷺ is established in this *dunyā*, then it continues in the Barzakh, and finally it reaches its apex in Dār al-Jazāʾ (the Final Abode of the

Afterlife). A person will be with those whom they love, namely in this life, in the next, and in the Eternal Garden. And even if they are not granted the vision of seeing him in this world, by His permission they will be greeted by him in the Barzakh, and will enjoy his companionship in Jannah for all of eternity.

Even if you feel unworthy while striving, know that your soul can still be honoured by his presence. So dare to hope, and dare to dream. If your soul can be blessed to witness the best of Allah's creation in your sleep, then what about the greatest of all rewards? What about seeing Allah Himself? That is the theme and topic of the next chapter.

"...so I may do good in what I left behind."
Never! It is only a [useless] appeal they make.
And there is a barrier [the Barzakh] behind
them until the Day they are resurrected.

AL-MU'MINŪN, 23:100

6

Is Allah speaking to you?

Have you ever seen Allah ﷻ? And if the answer is in the negative, how often do you speak to Him and address Him as if you can actually see Him? Every day, we open our eyes and behold the world's bounties: the beauty of creation, the faces we love, and the blessings we so often overlook. Sight is a powerful sense, a fact that is corroborated by the well-known maxim, "Seeing is believing." But have you ever seen your Lord? If not, how do you draw near to Him? The great ascetic Abū Yazīd al-Bustāmī ؒ once said, "I saw my Lord in a dream and asked Him:

يَا رَبِّ، كَيْفَ الطَّرِيقُ إِلَيْكَ؟

'O my Lord, how do I draw close to You?'

Allah ﷻ answered by stating:

أُتْرُكْ نَفْسَكَ وَتَعَالَ

'Leave yourself behind and come closer.'" [60]

Imam Aḥmad ibn Ḥanbal ﵀ also narrated a dream in which he saw Allah ﷻ and asked Him, "O my Lord, how do I attain nearness to You?" Allah replied by stating:

يَا أَحْمَدُ، بِكَلَامِي

"O Aḥmad, [closeness is attained] through My words."

Imam Aḥmad then asked, "With understanding or without?" And Allah responded: "With or without understanding."[61] This account entails that reciting the Qur'an—even without full comprehension—draws you near to Him. Though understanding and contemplation brings depth, every recitation of His words is honoured. Ibn al-Jawzī ﵀ narrated that Yaḥyā al-Bakkā' ﵀ once saw his Lord in a dream and said:

كَمْ أَدْعُوكَ وَلَا تُجِيبُنِي؟

"O my Lord, how long have I called upon You without receiving any response?"

---

60 Ibn al-Jawzi, *Sifat as-Safwa*, 2:306

61 Abu Hasan Ali, *at-Tabsira*, 2:269

Allah ﷻ said in response:

يَا يَحْيَىٰ، إِنِّي أُحِبُّ أَنْ أَسْمَعَ صَوْتَكَ

"O Yaḥyā, I love to hear your voice."[62]

The Prophet ﷺ taught us the definition of *iḥsān* (religious excellence): "That you worship Allah as though you can see Him. And if you cannot see Him, know that He sees you."[63] In one narration, he elaborated even further on this concept. The Companion Muʿādh ibn Jabal ؓ narrated, "I said, 'O Messenger of Allah, impart to me a piece of advice.'" He ﷺ replied: "I advise you to worship Allah as though you see Him, and count yourself among the already dead. Remember Allah near every stone and tree. If you commit a sin, follow it with a good deed in its place: a secret one for a secret wrong, and a public one for a public one."[64] Why pair worshipping Allah as though you see Him with counting yourself among the dead? This is because when you detach yourself from the illusions of this world, you begin to see the truth more clearly. And there is no truth more real than the Ultimate Truth: Allah. There are authentic narrations of some righteous predecessors claiming to have seen Allah in dreams. Among them is the great Imam Abū Ḥanīfah ؒ, who reportedly saw Allah multiple times during his life. These are visions of the heart, which are real in a spiritual sense, but not comparable to the

62 Ibn Jawzi, *Sayd al-Khatir*, 84

63 *Ṣaḥīḥ al-Bukhārī*, 10.

64 *Muṣannaf Ibn Abī Shaybah*, 37044.

Iḥsān (religious excellence) is to worship Allah as though you can see Him. When you detach yourself from the illusions of this world, you begin to see the truth more clearly. And there is no truth more real than the Ultimate Truth: Allah.

ultimate vision in the Hereafter. And that is the true gift we long for: to see Allah, not in sleep, but with our own eyes in Jannah in what is known as the Beatific Vision. Until then, speak to Him and address Him sincerely through the blessing of *duʿā'* (supplication). Recite His words, worship as though you see Him, and let your soul be drawn closer, step by step, until that day comes.

So why even explore and mention the topic of having dreams where one sees Allah? If one pays close attention to the few authentic reports that exist in this topic, it can be inferred that the path to nearness is through the Qur'an—His words—and through *duʿā'*, namely your words to Him. The main point is that you do not need to see Allah in this world to be connected to Him. In fact, you are already engaging with Him directly multiple times a day. Every time you raise your hands in supplication and every time you recite His words, you are in a direct conversation with your Lord. Yet, how many people speak about Allah, but never speak *to* Allah? How many people know about Allah, but never truly *know* Him? Recognising the reality of this direct engagement can transform the heart and reorient the soul. And anyone who has tasted that closeness naturally desires more. That is why the Prophet Mūsā ﷺ asked to see Allah in this world. But even when that request was denied, Allah honoured him with something greater: He made him Kalīm Allāh: the one whom Allah spoke to directly. And that, too, is a gift we can experience in part by speaking to Allah sincerely and spiritually engaging with His words through our hearts.

For, as Allah states in one of His explicit verses:

وَإِذَا سَأَلَكَ عِبَادِي عَنِّي فَإِنِّي قَرِيبٌ

"When My servants ask you about Me: I am truly near."[65]

Likewise, before humans even physically existed and only subsisted in the metaphysical plane, they were all directly addressed by Allah:

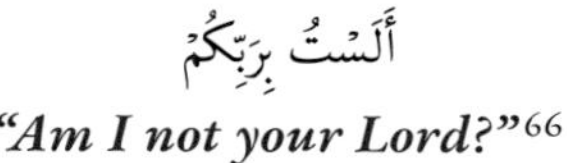

"Am I not your Lord?"[66]

You possess all this time—between now and that Day—to obtain knowledge of Him. Will you be ready to answer the questions when they come? The believer speaks to Allah more than anyone else in their life. Just in *ṣalāh* (prayer) alone, a person recites Sūrah al-Fātiḥah at least 17 times a day. And every single time, Allah responds to His servant's address directly. Even without praying a single Sunnah or supererogatory prayer, a person is still engaged in a direct, personal conversation with their Lord multiple times a day. It is for this reason that a popular aphorism attributed to some of the righteous states:

ٱلصَّلَاةُ مِعْرَاجُ ٱلْمُؤْمِنِ

"Prayer is the ascension of the believer."[67]

---

65 *al-Baqarah*, 2:186.

66 *al-A'rāf*, 7:172.

67 Muhammad ibn Ibrāhīm al-Tuwayjirī, *Mawsū'ah Fiqh al-Qulūb*, vol. 3, 2795.

Just as Allah took the Prophet ﷺ on the Night Journey—in the form of both body and soul—and legislated the prayer directly to him, He has gifted us the *ṣalāh* as our own journey, where the soul ascends and the heart connects with the Creator. The Prophet said: "The closest that a servant is to his Lord is in the state of *sujūd* (prostration)."[68] On one occasion, a man who had embraced Islam issuing the following reply when he was asked what moved him the most about Islam and caused him to convert: "I never knew God could be so accessible. I never imagined I could talk to Him directly." And the Prophet ﷺ said that Allah says in a Hadith Qudsī:

أَنَا مَعَ عَبْدِي إِذَا هُوَ ذَكَرَنِي وَتَحَرَّكَتْ بِي شَفَتَاهُ

"I am with My servant when he remembers Me, and his lips move with My name."[69]

Thus, while it is true that seeing Allah is the greatest reward in the Hereafter, speaking to Him, remembering Him, and calling upon Him constitute the gateway to that final destination. Such pathways remain open to the believer who is heedful of their Lord.

You will not mention Allah except that He will mention you as well. And your soul—whether you realise it or not—longs for Him at every moment. This is the case even during your sleep. Imam al-Bayhaqī ﵀ narrates a report attributed to Abū al-Dardā' ﵁

68 *Ṣaḥīḥ Muslim*, 482.

69 *Sunan Ibn Mājah*, 3792.

and a similar narration from ʿAbdullāh ibn ʿAmr ﵁, wherein both state that the soul of the believer is brought to the Throne of Allah when he sleeps; if he slept in a state of *ṭahārah* (ritual purity), his soul is permitted to make *sujūd* to Allah.[70] The Sunnah encourages us to perform *wuḍū'* (ablution) before sleeping. And we know that if we do so, the Angels will then make *duʿā'* for us throughout the night. So even as your body rests, your soul is drawn near to the divine. And if your final deed before sleep was a virtuous one—namely being in a state of *wuḍū'*—then that goodness continues to shape your soul's journey through the night. The depth of your longing for Allah shapes how quickly and how profoundly your soul will encounter Him in the Barzakh.

Has anyone already seen Allah? Of course, nothing in this life compares to the ultimate Beatific Vision of Him in the Hereafter. But we have narrations that provide us a glimpse into that nearness. Consider the narration of Jābir ﵁, who said: "The Prophet ﷺ came to me after my father was martyred at Uḥud and said:

يَا جَابِرُ، مَا لِي أَرَاكَ مُنْكَسِرًا؟

'O Jābir, why do I see you so broken-hearted?'"

Jābir ﵁ replied, "O Messenger of Allah, my father has been killed. He left behind many dependents and many debts." The Prophet said: "Shall I not give you good tidings? No one has ever spoken to Allah directly except from behind a veil.

70 Ibn Hajar, *Fath al-Bari*

But as for your father, Allah spoke to him directly. And Allah said to him:

يَا عَبْدِي، تَمَنَّ عَلَيَّ أُعْطِكَ

'O My servant, ask Me anything and I will give it to you.'

He said:

يَا رَبِّ، أَحْيِنِي فَأُقْتَلَ فِيكَ ثَانِيَةً

'My Lord, bring me back to life so I may be martyred again for Your sake.'

But Allah responded:

إِنَّهُ، سَبَقَ مِنِّي أَنَّهُمْ إِلَيْهَا لَا يَرْجِعُونَ

'It has already been decreed that they shall not return to this world.'

So the martyr said:

يَا رَبِّ، فَأَبْلِغْ مَنْ وَرَائِي

'Then, my Lord, inform those that have been left behind.'

And it was then that Allah revealed:

وَلَا تَحْسَبَنَّ ٱلَّذِينَ قُتِلُوا۟ فِى سَبِيلِ ٱللَّهِ أَمْوَٰتًا بَلْ أَحْيَآءٌ عِندَ رَبِّهِمْ يُرْزَقُونَ

'Never think of those martyred in the cause of Allah as dead. In fact, they are alive with their Lord, well provided for.'[71]"[72]

---

71 *Āl ʿImrān*, 3:169.

72 *Sunan al-Tirmidhī*, 3010.

The only blessing that this martyr wanted after speaking to Allah face-to-face was to come back just so that they could sacrifice their life for Him again. Now, think of the martyrs of Gaza, Yemen, and of every corner of the Ummah longing not just to see Allah, but to strive for Him over and over again. Consider Imam Aḥmad ﵀, who endured so much torture for the sake of the truth. During his ordeal, the Prophet ﷺ would be seen in the dreams of others comforting him. And after his death, a student said: "I saw Imam Aḥmad in a dream. I asked, 'O Abu ʿAbdullāh, what did your Lord do with you?' He said, 'He forgave me. And He said to me: "O Aḥmad, you took sixty lashes for My sake." I replied, "Yes, my Lord." He said, "Then look upon My Face as much as you wish."'"[73] One thus infers that there is a connection between an unseen sacrifice in this world and the ultimate reward of seeing Allah in the next. And while that direct vision of Allah is reserved for Jannah, in this world you can still witness His signs. When you die, another veil is lifted, and your soul will perceive what was always there, but hidden.

When we die, every soul sees what it truly earned. The disbelievers are met by Angels of torment and punishment. Conversely, the believers are welcomed by Angels of mercy. And the *shuhadā'* (martyrs) see Paradise from the very first strike. As for the believing soul, it experiences its own version of al-Isrā' wal-Miʿrāj, namely a journey of ascent toward Allah. Imam al-Ḍaḥḥāk ﵀ narrated: "When the soul of the believing

73 Al-Baghdadi, *Tarikh Baghdad*, 6:90

If you long for the gift of beholding Allah with your own eyes in the Hereafter, know that He has already given you access to Him in this life. The path to Him is through His Book, *ṣalāh*, and *du'ā'*.

servant is taken, it is raised to the heavens. And those nearest to Allah accompany it, saying, 'O Lord, this is Your servant, so-and-so', even though Allah knows best. Then Allah sends down a sealed certificate which provides him a guarantee of safety from punishment." This is the very meaning and theme found in Sūrah al-Muṭaffifīn:

كَلَّآ إِنَّ كِتَابَ ٱلْأَبْرَارِ لَفِى عِلِّيِّينَ وَمَآ أَدْرَىٰكَ مَا عِلِّيُّونَ كِتَـٰبٌ مَّرْقُومٌ يَشْهَدُهُ ٱلْمُقَرَّبُونَ

"But no! The virtuous are certainly bound for 'Illiyyīn [in elevated Gardens], and what will make you realise what 'Illiyyīn is? A fate sealed, witnessed by those nearest [to Allah]."[74]

The ultimate question is whether you can see Allah now through His signs and His verses. Do the *āyāt* (signs of the divine) around you sharpen your spiritual vision? Or are you waiting for the universe to collapse around you, that is, only to see clearly when it is too late to act? If you long for the gift of beholding Him with your own eyes in the Hereafter, know that He has already given you access to Him in this life. The path to Him is through His Book, *ṣalāh*, and *du'ā'*. Will you wait to see Him only there, or will you strive to come closer to Him here, so that your vision is already focused before that final veil is lifted in the other world?

74 *al-Muṭaffifīn*, 83:18–21.

7

How many lives do you really have?

When you carefully look in the mirror, you may see a living human being. But what is really found on the other side of that reflection? Are you truly alive, or are you just a corpse in waiting? You may have fed your body in a physical sense, but have you starved your soul and left it unnourished at the metaphysical level? How many times have you killed your own spiritual heart? And how many times can it be brought back to life? Imam Ibn Qayyim al-Jawziyyah ﵀ narrates that Allah ﷻ revealed to Prophet Mūsā ﵇ the following words:

يَا مُوسَى إِنَّ أَوَّلَ مَن مَاتَ مِنْ خَلْقِي إِبْلِيسُ، وَذَلِكَ أَنَّهُ أَوَّلُ مَنْ عَصَانِي،
وَإِنَّما أَعُدُّ مَنْ عَصَانِي مِنَ الأَمْواتِ

"O Mūsā, the first member of My creation to truly die was Iblīs, for he disobeyed Me. And I count the one who disobeys Me to be among the dead." [75]

By contrast, in the Islamic tradition, the great Companion 'Umar ﷺ is described as a dead man that was brought back to life. Allah states:

أَوَمَنْ كَانَ مَيْتًا فَأَحْيَيْنَاهُ وَجَعَلْنَا لَهُ نُورًا يَمْشِي بِهِ فِي النَّاسِ

"...those who had been dead, to whom We gave life and a light with which they can walk among people..." [76]

Imagine seeing 'Umar ﷺ before Islam: indulging in alcohol, inflicting harm on his competitors and rivals, and even plotting to kill the Prophet ﷺ. Then imagine seeing 'Umar ﷺ after Islam as the Khalīfah of the Muslim nation, walking with the light of guidance. The latter iteration is not the same human being: one was spiritually dead, while the other was brought to life.

In Sūrah al-Ḥadīd, Allah says:

أَلَمْ يَأْنِ لِلَّذِينَ آمَنُوا أَنْ تَخْشَعَ قُلُوبُهُمْ لِذِكْرِ اللَّهِ وَمَا نَزَلَ مِنَ الْحَقِّ

"Has the time not yet come for believers' hearts to be humbled at the remembrance of Allah and what has been revealed of the truth?" [77]

---

75 Ibn Qayyim al-Jawziyyah, *al-Dā' wa al-Dawā'*, 127.

76 *al-An'ām*, 6:122.

77 *al-Ḥadīd*, 57:16.

Then, immediately after asking this rhetorical question, He says:

اِعْلَمُوا أَنَّ اللَّهَ يُحْيِ الْأَرْضَ بَعْدَ مَوْتِهَا

"Know that Allah revives the earth after its death."[78]

Through this powerful metaphor, Allah signifies that no matter how dead your heart or soul may feel, it can still be revived once more. Your body might be physically alive, but are you truly living in a spiritual sense? That depends entirely on the state of your soul. Some members of the *salaf* (pious predecessors) used to say: "The death of the heart is far more frightening than the death of the body." Furthermore, the Prophet said that the most truthful line of poetry is the following composed by Labīd ibn Rabīʿah ﷺ:

أَلَا كُلُّ شَيْءٍ مَا خَلَا اللَّهَ بَاطِلُ

"Without any doubt, everything except Allah is devoid of value."[79]

This principle even includes your physical body if it is not connected to Allah. Your physical life moves through several stages: 1) ʿĀlam al-Dharr: the realm of pre-existence, when you were only a soul; 1) Ḥayāh al-Dunyā: this worldly life, where body and soul are fused, forming the *nafs* (self); 3) al-Barzakh: the phase after death, where the soul lives on while the body

78 *al-Ḥadīd*, 57:17.

79 *Ṣaḥīḥ al-Bukhārī*, 3841.

returns to the earth; 4) the Ākhirah: when Allah will resurrect you, causing rain to descend, whereby from the *ʿajb al-dhanab* (the coccyx, which is a minuscule part of the tailbone) a new body will sprout and reunite with the soul. This body-soul pairing will then entail eternal consequences once it is resurrected. But here there is a crucial distinction: your body only lives once. Your soul can be brought back to life over and over again, a fact that makes this journey so powerful. A person may die at 80 years old but, at the spiritual level, they may only be 8 days old. Because it was only then—after all the layers of sin, heedlessness, or hardship—that they truly returned to Allah. Every act of repentance, every sincere moment of *dhikr* (divine remembrance), and every tear shed in *sujūd* (prostration) strips away the old version of you. What remains is a fresh, living, and awakened believer that is reborn not in body, but in spirit.

The journey of the believer is one of constant rebirth, a process that does not occur just once in a lifetime, but over and over again. The process of rejuvenation occurs through every sincere moment of return, every act of devotion, and every struggle against the self. Every time you sincerely turn back to Allah, you are spiritually reborn. The Prophet ﷺ described this phenomenon vividly in many Hadiths, showing us how Allah continually gives us the opportunity to start anew with a fresh slate, just like the day we entered this world. For instance, the Prophet ﷺ said that when a Muslim performs *wuḍūʾ* (ablution) properly and stands in prayer with presence, fully knowing what they are saying, they finish that *ṣalāh* (prayer) as pure as the day their mother gave birth to them.[80] Just as a newborn infant enters the world wrapped in amniotic fluid, the believer emerges from *ṣalāh* wrapped in the mercy and forgiveness of Allah. Even the small actions within the prayer symbolise the same process of purification; for instance, when you bow and prostrate, sins fall off like sand would fall from the back and shoulders, as related in a Hadith from the Prophet ﷺ.[81]

And that connection does not simply apply to the *ṣalāh*. The Prophet ﷺ mentioned that the Angels in the Highest Assembly were arguing about the best of deeds with respect to their ability to expiate a person's sins, and he was informed of this scene in a dream. In this vision, Allah Himself asked the Prophet ﷺ what those deeds were. The Prophet ﷺ responded correctly to this query, after having knowledge placed in his chest by Allah; he explained that whoever does these acts will live well, die well, and be purified like the day they were born. He noted that the deeds which expiate one's sins in their entirety are 1) walking to the *masjid* for the congregational prayers, 2) making *wuḍū'* in difficult conditions, and 3) waiting for the next prayer.[82]

The process of spiritual rebirth comes with effort, just like physical birth. There is certainly a strong degree of discomfort, waiting, and pain, but what follows is a new life. A baby is carried for nine months and then delivered with tears and struggle. The soul, too, carries the burden of sins until it delivers them to Allah in repentance, and then it is

80 *Musnad al-Dārimī*, 743.

81 *Ṣaḥīḥ Ibn Hibbān*, 1743.

82 *Sunan al-Tirmidhī*, 3233.

born again. Even Hajj, the pinnacle of physical and spiritual striving, is described by the Prophet ﷺ as a return to the state of complete purity. A person who performs Hajj without corruption or argumentation returns back to their home like a newborn, whereby they are completely forgiven.

A vivid observation that is worthy of reflection is how everything about Hajj mirrors the process of birth. You stand on ʿArafah, which is the very place where your soul once stood before it came into this world, renewing your covenant with Allah. Then you move to Muzdalifah, the symbolic resting place of the souls. After that, you re-enter the world and commence your presence within it by stoning the Shayṭān, a moment that draws parallels with the starting point of your actual birth, where Shayṭān poked you. But this time, in your spiritual rebirth, you stone him instead. You then offer your *uḍḥiyyah* (sacrificial animal) at the culmination of the Hajj. At the point of your physical birth, your parents arranged a sacrifice on your behalf, which is known as the *ʿaqīqah*. But this time, as a spiritually awakened soul, you offer it yourself for the sake of Allah. After that, you proceed to perform the *ṭawāf* (circumambulation), placing Allah at the centre of your life as you circle the Kaʿbah. You proceed to then perform the act of *al-saʿy* (ambulation), symbolising your dependence on Allah in all of your affairs, just as Hājar did when she ran between Ṣafā and Marwah. Eventually, you exit your state of *iḥrām*, which closely resembles your *kafan* (burial shroud) that will be put on you after you pass away. It symbolises the moment of death and preparation to meet your Lord. Then, you celebrate ʿĪd with the believers, echoing the joyful reunion and celebration of the believers in Jannah. In just a few days, Ḥajj becomes a complete simulation of life, death, and rebirth, and in sum, a chance for the soul to be reborn entirely. The journey of pilgrimage in this world acts as a spiritual rebirth, because it reflects the greater journey of the Ākhirah (Afterlife).

But that kind of rebirth does not only happen in Mecca; in fact, it happens in other sacred journeys too, like the one to al-Masjid al-Aqṣā, a place that holds deep meaning for the hearts of the believers. The Prophet ﷺ said that when the Prophet Sulaymān completed the construction of Bayt al-Maqdis, he asked Allah for three things: 1) judgment aligned with divine wisdom, 2) a kingdom like no other, and 3) that anyone who visits it with the sole purpose of praying within its perimeter would emerge pure of sin, just like the day their mother gave birth to them. And the Prophet ﷺ said the first two wishes were granted, and he hoped the third was as well.[83]

Moreover, there is the sacred journey of the Hijrah, namely a migration that is done for the sake of Allah. In this case, a person literally leaves behind their old life, their old sins, and begins their life with a fresh slate in a new land for the sake of their Lord. And Allah allows those sins to remain in the place they left behind, while they start over with a clean record. There is also the powerful form of rebirth that comes through gratitude in times of trial. In a notable Hadith, the Companion

---

83 *Sunan Ibn Mājah*, 1408.

Shaddād ibn Aws narrated that he heard the Prophet ﷺ say that Allah said in a Hadith Qudsī: "When I test a believing servant of Mine, and he praises Me for what I tested him with, then he will rise up that day just like the day his mother gave birth to him."[84] This is because sins fall off in the midst of hardships, especially when the servant praises Allah during the trial. The greater the hardship, the greater the expiation and reward. To reflect on all these forms of spiritual rebirth, consider the words of Imam al-Ghazālī, who said: "What is rebirth and death anyway except for a transition from one state to another?" Whether you are embracing Islam, performing Hajj, making Hijrah, or enduring a hardship with *ṣabr* (patience) and *ḥamd* (praise of Allah), each moment is a spiritual migration and stepping stone towards a new phase of nearness to Allah.

Every day that you are currently living constitutes a golden opportunity to reinvent yourself, to awaken the heart inside of you, and to even be spiritually reborn. But when your moment of physical death comes, and you are literally reborn, your chance for spiritual rebirth is officially over. Because once the latter event occurs, you will be closing the casing of your body and this world altogether. Paradoxically, your death is your new life at the next station, based on the life you are leading and choosing to carve in this station. Death is a new birth, a type of transfer from one state to another that humans do not take lightly. This is because it is understandably traumatic and

84 *Musnad Aḥmad*, 17118.

painful to move from one dimension to another, which is part of the wisdom in the *du'ā'* of Yaḥyā and 'Īsā ﷺ:

وَالسَّلَامُ عَلَيَّ يَوْمَ وُلِدتُّ وَيَوْمَ أَمُوتُ وَيَوْمَ أُبْعَثُ حَيًّا

"Peace be upon me the day I was born, the day I die, and the day I will be brought back to life."[85]

It is in those pivotal moments and transitions that you feel the greatest compression. In this context, one could think about a baby whose mother has gestational diabetes or is exceptionally large for any other reason, and how difficult it is for that child to enter this world. Similar to this, a soul that is inflated with ego and sin will be overburdened and weighed down by its sins when it must go to the other world. For the believer, the transition at first sight seems difficult, but once the appointed time comes, it passes with relative ease. As Imam al-Ghazālī ﷺ says, at first the pious ones find the transfer discomforting—just like the baby hates coming into this world—because it feels like it is being pulled away from the warmth of the womb and the nourishment it was receiving. But once the baby is comfortable, it grows to love this world and would never want to return to its mother's womb or enter the grave. Likewise, the believer—after that initial process of birth into the Barzakh—begins to love that next world more than anything else, after the first squeeze and separation. But just like when you came into this life, there is a constriction, a point of labour, and an entrance through a narrow passage. And the few hours of birth—in this case, death—can feel like an eternity.

85 *Maryam*, 19:15, 19:33.

Will you wait for that fateful day to arrive—when your soul leaves this world—to discover whether you were spiritually alive in the first place? Or will you make the effort to revive your soul here and now, so that when you exit into the Barzakh, your rebirth will be into a world of light and life? And what if, despite all your efforts to be reborn, your faith still feels like it is flickering and descending? The path to the gate of the next world is a laborious transition, and the only way to make it through is to hold on tightly and make the necessary spiritual preparations ahead of time.

"...so I may do good in what I left behind." Never! It is only a [useless] appeal they make. And there is a barrier [the Barzakh] behind them until the Day they are resurrected.

AL-MU'MINŪN, 23:100

What does it feel like when you die?

There is no doubt that the stages and phases of life can be overwhelming. At times, they pull you in every direction. No matter how much you try to stay grounded, trials can continue to compress you and feel unsurmountable. While temptations tug from one side, hardships and tribulations come from the other. Exhaustion and frustration weigh heavily, and it may feel like you cannot proceed any further. But pause and look within yourself with your inner introspective 'sight'. There is a firm and unbreakable rope that is stretched before you. It is your anchor and your means of survival. But it is your obligation to firmly hold onto it so that you remain grounded in your faith. Qays ibn ʿAbbād ﷺ once said: "I was in the *masjid* when a humble, devout, and upright man entered. He performed two *rakʿahs* (units) of prayer. The people around me whispered, 'That is ʿAbdullāh ibn Salām, a man from the people of Jannah.' So I approached him afterwards and asked, 'Are you the one they say is from the people of Jannah?' He replied, '*Subḥānallāh* (Glory be to Allah)! People should not speak about what they do not know. But I did have a dream during the time of the Prophet ﷺ.'"

ʿAbdullāh ibn Salām ﷺ, the former chief rabbi of Medina who embraced Islam and became one of the great scholars of the early Muslim community, then described his dream: "During the time of the Prophet ﷺ, I saw myself in a beautiful and vast garden. At its centre stood a tall pole, and at the top was a handhold. I was told to climb it and hold onto it. But I asked how I could possibly reach it. Suddenly, an Angel lifted me upward like a strong wind, and I reached the top and grabbed the handhold. I awoke while still firmly holding onto it. I then went to the Prophet ﷺ and asked him about the dream. He ﷺ said, 'As for the garden, it is the Garden of Islam. As for the pole, it is the pillar of Islam. As for the handhold, it is the *al-ʿurwah al-wuthqā* (firm grip of faith) that Allah mentions in the Qur'an.' Then the Prophet ﷺ said, 'You will remain upon Islam until you die.'"[86]

86 *Ṣaḥīḥ Muslim*, 2484.

Hold on to the rope of Allah with strength, patience, and certainty. While everything in this world calls you to let go, your salvation lies in holding firm to His rope.

Allah reminds us repeatedly to hold firm and to never let go of *al-ʿurwah al-wuthqā* because the world's evil devices will deceive and pull us away from the truth. In a parallel fashion, He also issues to the Ummah the following command:

وَاعْتَصِمُوا بِحَبْلِ اللَّهِ جَمِيعًا

"And hold firmly together to the rope of Allah."[87]

This is because division weakens us and strips away His divine favour. He also tells us in another verse:

خُذُوا مَا آتَيْنَاكُمْ بِقُوَّة

"Hold firmly to that [Scripture] which We have given you."[88]

This imperative serves as a reminder that Islam is not a casual or part-time commitment that can be loosened whenever it is deemed convenient. Becoming lackadaisical in one's religious commitment is a dangerous undertaking, since a person is likely to slip and trek the path of moral decay. When hearts become careless, deception seeps in. The Prophet ﷺ warned that a time would come when patience would be like holding onto a blazing and burning coal.[89] Through another striking figure of speech, he instructed us to cling to his Sunnah, firmly biting down upon it with our molar teeth.[90] This is because there will be times of confusion and trial such that the truth

87 *Āl ʿImrān*, 3:103.

88 *al-Baqarah*, 2:63.

89 *Sunan al-Tirmidhī*, 2260.

90 *Sunan al-Tirmidhī*, 2676.

will be corrupted. Without the Sunnah, a person may easily drift into misguidance. In another report echoing the same theme, the Prophet ﷺ also praised the man who is called to *zinā* (illegal sexual intercourse) by a woman of beauty and status, but he turns away from that moment of temptation and says, "Indeed, I fear Allah."[91] For restraining himself in that moment of intense temptation, Allah will grant him the shade of His Throne on the Day of Judgment. Furthermore, the Prophet ﷺ said, "The greatest jihad is to speak a word of truth in front of a tyrant."[92] The person who stands up to the tyrant does so without fearing their wrath and punishment, and instead remains resolute and steadfast upon the truth. So hold on to the rope of Allah with strength, patience, and certainty. While everything in this world calls you to let go, your salvation lies in holding firm to His rope.

Just imagine the brave Companion ʿAbdullāh ibn Ḥudhāfah ﷺ and how he would stand in the courtyards of powerful tyrants, fearless and unwavering, speaking words of truth without any hesitation. Then picture the other noble Companions who faced the most brutal rulers of their time, not with weapons, but with conviction and courage. Now think of the brave men and women of Gaza, who—despite daily oppression—stand firm in their belief in the One and put their trust in Him alone, thereby refusing to bow to tyranny. Some may lose their lives not because they are weak, but precisely

91 *Ṣaḥīḥ al-Bukhārī*, 660.

92 *Sunan Abī Dāwūd*, 4344.

because they are unshaken by the pressure of the thrones they stand before. Yet, their souls ascend quickly not to the thrones of this world, but to the Throne of the Most Merciful, where they roam freely in the gardens of Paradise. That moment of pressure passes quickly.

There is no greater pressure in this life than the moment of death. That explains why the Prophet would frequently recite the following supplication:

يَا مُقَلِّبَ الْقُلُوبِ، ثَبِّتْ قَلْبِي عَلَى دِينِكَ

"O Turner of hearts, make my heart firm (thabbit qalbī) upon Your religion."[93]

Reflect on the word *thabāt* (firmness) and its linguistic meaning. This word and its cognates are found in many proof texts of our religion. For instance, Allah says in the Qur'an:

يُثَبِّتُ اللَّهُ الَّذِينَ آمَنُوا بِالْقَوْلِ الثَّابِتِ فِي الْحَيَاةِ الدُّنْيَا وَفِي الْآخِرَةِ

"Allah makes the believers steadfast (yuthabbit Allāh) with the firm Word [of faith] in this worldly life and the Hereafter."[94]

---

93 *Sunan al-Tirmidhī*, 3522.

94 *Ibrāhīm*, 14:27.

In the final moments of life, when the pain of death intensifies, and the devils surround a person for one last attempt to lead them astray, it is the one who held firm throughout their life who will still say, "*Lā ilāha illa Allāh* (there is no God except Allah)." Note here that the Prophet ﷺ did not limit his *duʿā'* (supplication) for firmness to this life only; this is because the time when you will need *thabāt* most is when the Angels descend into your grave to question you about your faith, your Lord, and your Prophet. That moment will be more terrifying than facing any worldly tyrant. As such, the Prophet ﷺ said: "When you bury your brother or sister, ask Allah to grant them firmness."[95] This is because the most difficult test of their existence is about to begin, as they will be questioned by Munkar and Nakīr. And the fact of the matter is that you do not know when your test will come. Just as you rehearse the processes of death and resurrection each day by sleeping and waking, every moment that you face pressure over your faith is a rehearsal for that final trial. Every time that you say "*Lā ilāha illa Allāh*" in times of pressure or duress, you are essentially training your soul for the ultimate moment and greatest test that will come after your last breath. Allah says:

وَمَا تَدْرِي نَفْسٌ مَّاذَا تَكْسِبُ غَدًاۖ وَمَا تَدْرِي نَفْسٌۢ بِأَيِّ أَرْضٍ تَمُوتُ

"No soul knows what it will earn for tomorrow, and no soul knows in what land it will die."[96]

95 *Sunan Abī Dāwūd*, 3221.

96 *Luqmān*, 31:34.

You cannot prepare for the test of death in the final decisive moments of life, because you do not know when or where it will come. The appointment for your soul's departure is known only to Allah. Imam al-Qurṭubī ﷺ expressed this subtle point beautifully and poetically by saying:

> ***"We walk the paths that fate has drawn,***
> ***And those destined to walk shall carry on.***
> ***Our sustenance is scattered far and wide,***
> ***But what is ours will not be denied.***
> ***If death is written in a land,***
> ***In no other place shall we make our last stand."***[97]

Each one of us has a land in which our soul will leave this world, yet we do not know where it is. The Prophet ﷺ said that when the appointed time comes, Allah Himself creates a need for you in that very location to facilitate the soul extraction process.[98] And when you happen to arrive at your final destination, the Angel of Death—who is known as Malak al-Mawt in Arabic—will be waiting. In this regard, Imam al-Qurṭubī ﷺ narrated a striking story about the Prophet Sulaymān ﷺ. One day, a man came to him and said, "O Prophet of Allah, I have an urgent need in India. Can you command the wind to carry me there immediately?" Sulaymān ﷺ complied and honoured his request. But then he noticed the Angel of Death smiling. He asked him, "Why

97 Al-Qurtubi, *at-Tadhkirah*, 1:294

98 *Sunan al-Tirmidhī*, 2147.

are you smiling?" The Angel of Death replied, "I was amazed, since I was commanded to take this man's soul in India at the end of this very hour. But I saw him standing here with you."[99] And indeed, the wind carried him to India within the hour, and that was where his soul was taken. This is the reality of life and death: your time may come at the most unexpected moment and at the most unexpected place. And when it does, it is hoped that Allah will make us among those whose hearts remain firm and content with His religion.

At the moment of death, you lift your gaze and there, before your eyes, are Angels descending. Whether they approach you with mercy or wrath depends on the life you lived. These are the same Angels who once breathed your soul into your body, and now, they have come to take it back. The Prophet ﷺ said that for the believing soul, Angels descend while being clothed in light, appearing on the horizon, and filling the view with serenity. The Angel of Death approaches while carrying a *kafan* (shroud) from Paradise that is scented with musk. And they say to the believer whose appointed time has come: "Peace be upon you. Do not be afraid, O pure soul. Come forth to the mercy and pleasure of Allah."[100] In a state of contentedness, your soul rushes eagerly from your body with a smile, as smoothly as the last drop of water from a jug. You see it ascend, wrapped in the perfumed shroud, longing to meet its Lord Who is most pleased with it.

---

99 Nilofar Ahmed, "Islam's Concept of Death," *Dawn*, October 21, 2010, https://www.dawn.com/news/574590/islam-s-concept-of-death-by-nilofar-ahmed.

100 *Musnad Aḥmad*, 18557.

Angels who once breathed your soul into your body, at death, they come to take it back. For the believing soul, angels descend while being clothed in light, appearing on the horizon, and filling the view with serenity.

As for the wicked soul, the Angels descend with fury and darkness. They shout in harshness, and the soul tries to hide within the body. The Angel of Death rips it out with a sharp hook which is as violent as the process of tearing through wet wool. They say: "Come out to the anger of a Lord you ignored, and to the consequences you hoped were not real." This is the moment to hold tightly to *lā ilāha illa Allāh*, which is the word of *thabāt*. Because this is the most severe moment of your existence before the Day of Judgment. On one occasion, an Angel placed your soul into the womb, and after months of labor, you emerged into this world with a painful squeeze. Now, your soul is taken again, either gently to the heavens for comfort and reward, or to the abyss of Sijjīn, the lowest depths where ruined souls are discarded.

And then begins your rebirth in the realm of Barzakh. You return to the earth, just as Allah promised in His Book. The Prophet ﷺ described the squeeze of the grave, which is distinct from the punishment of the grave, which is reserved for sinners. Even Saʿd ibn Muʿādh ؓ, whose death shook the Throne of Allah, was not spared from it. Nor is a pure infant who never lived long enough to sin is saved from this trial. Every soul—even those of the righteous—must feel that initial point of constriction. For some, it is brief like a gentle squeeze during birth. For people weighed down by sins and faults, their ribs are crushed within it.

After this, the test of one's true purpose commences. There were two Angels—namely Raqīb and ʿAtīd—who recorded your deeds. Now, there will be two other Angels, Munkar and Nakīr, who will question you. And when you rise on the Day of Judgment, you will be met by two other Angels appointed by Allah: Sā'iq and Shahīd. Even the appearance of the Angels who come to you will reflect the life you lived. This means that Munkar and Nakīr will appear beautiful to the righteous, but terrifying to the wicked. Your deeds will shape and determine their form. Then the real test begins; in a thunderous voice, they will ask:

مَنْ رَبُّكَ؟ مَا دِينُكَ؟ مَنْ نَبِيُّكَ؟

"Who is your Lord? What is your religion? Who is your Prophet?"[101]

In that moment, you will not be able to manufacture answers spontaneously. You will only utter what your soul has been attuned to say through your intrinsic nature and inclination. If your heart was firm in this life and obedient to the dictates of Islam, it will remain firm then. If you lived by the values of *lā ilāha illa Allāh*, you will respond in accordance with its teachings effortlessly. But if you were negligent towards fulfilling your religious duties, your tongue will falter. Panic and confusion will silence you. And as such, it is imperative to hold on tight to the teachings of Islam. Let the remembrance of Allah settle your soul now, so it can remain settled then. If you remain firm, the labour of death will pass, the grave will become a garden, and your soul will transition smoothly into the next life, where it will be at peace and honoured.

---

101 *Sunan Abī Dāwūd*, 4753.

9

When you meet the souls of Gaza

Have you ever wondered whether there is justice in the Barzakh? How many nights have you laid awake, helpless and restless, because of cowards hiding behind power and weaponry? In this world, there are many monsters in suits, launching bombs without shame or consequence. How much more sleep do you think is stolen from the men, women, and children whose lives are shattered, burned, broken, and tortured by the hands of the devils in human form? How many times have you looked at tyrants and wished they were the ones who could not sleep at night?

فَلَا نَامَتْ عَيْنُ الْجُبَانُ

"May the eye of the coward never sleep."[102]

These were the final words of Khālid ibn al-Walīd ﷺ when he was at his deathbed. Though he uttered these words in a battle-related—and hence worldly—context, it is hard not to feel the same today when we find tyrants go unchallenged and the innocent bleed in silence. And you may ask yourself: Am I wrong for wanting to see the oppressors taste even a portion of the pain that they have inflicted on innocent people? The answer is that such a disposition is natural, since it reflects a yearning for justice. You want to believe that the martyrs are comforted. In addition, you seek mental assurance that those who killed them will face consequences. Against the backdrop of such consequences, grief and anger are human emotions; even the Prophet ﷺ—who was the epitome of mercy—invoked the divine wrath of Allah against those who turned the earth into a place of slaughter. And here is where the Barzakh—life after death but before resurrection—offers both comfort and closure.

Once the soul reaches the point of death and traverses to the Barzakh, justice has already begun. On the night before the Battle of Yamāmah, where more than a thousand Muslims were killed, some of the Companions saw remarkable dreams. ʿAbbād ibn Bishr ﷺ, awoke saying: "I saw the heavens open, and

102 Ibn al-Jawzī, *Ṣifah al-Ṣafwah*, vol. 1, 654.

my soul ascended into them. Then they closed behind me."[103] After some reflection and contemplation, it appeared that he knew his appointed time had come. Ṭufayl ibn 'Amr ﷺ saw something even more profound. He dreamt that he was beheaded, and from his mouth emerged a bird that flew to a woman, who took it into her womb. Meanwhile, his son ran after him, but he could not reach him. Ṭufayl interpreted this dream as signifying his own martyrdom. The bird was his soul, the woman was the earth where he would be buried, and his son—who joined him in the battle—would survive, left behind to wonder what happened.[104] The way he interpreted his dream turned out to be fully accurate: Ṭufayl was beheaded, his son survived, and 'Abbād's body was mutilated to the extent that it was only identifiable by a sole birthmark.

Why is it necessary to recount these vivid scenes from history? The sobering fact is that many of us have witnessed far worse events over the past year. We have seen more graphic episodes of death, more violated bodies, and more beheaded children than we ever thought we would. And now, in places like Gaza, even the children use flowers in their artwork to symbolise the martyrs whose heads were taken. How many Ṭufayls are there in Gaza? How many 'Abbāds? How many of the righteous have now joined the very Companions they once read about? And just like Ṭufayl's son, we are left behind grieving, searching, and asking the following questions: Where are

103 Ibn Sa'd, *Tabaqat*, 3:441

104 al-Dhahabī, *Siyar A'lām al-Nubalā'*, vol. 1, 345-346.

our martyrs now? What is the fate of their souls? We find the answers to these questions from our religion. The Prophet ﷺ told us that when the martyrs of Uḥud died—many of whom were disfigured—Allah placed their souls in the bodies of green birds. They are able to fly freely through the gardens of Paradise, drink from its rivers, eat from its fruits, and rest in golden chandeliers suspended beneath the Throne of Allah.[105] After their deaths, Allah spoke to them directly, such that they were comforted. But even then, their concern was not just for themselves. They asked Allah: "Who will inform our families that we are alive, that we are being provided for, such that they do not lose faith in the struggle?" And Allah replied to them: "I will inform them on your behalf." They did not just want their loved ones to be comforted, but they wanted them to be inspired, such that they know that their sacrifices were not in vain, that the blood spilled was not forgotten, and that divine justice is already unfolding with certainty. To honour the martyrs of Uḥud and to strengthen the faith of their living relatives, Allah revealed the following Qur'anic verse:

وَلَا تَحْسَبَنَّ ٱلَّذِينَ قُتِلُوا فِي سَبِيلِ ٱللَّهِ أَمْوَاتًا ۚ بَلْ أَحْيَاءٌ عِندَ رَبِّهِمْ يُرْزَقُونَ

"Never think of those martyred in the cause of Allah as dead. In fact, they are alive with their Lord, well provided for."[106]

105 *Ṣaḥīḥ Muslim*, 1887.

106 *Āl 'Imrān*, 3:169.

The martyrs of Uḥud—and by extension the martyrs of Gaza—desire for us to know that they are well. Although they may no longer be with us, they have not ceased to exist. Rather, they are alive in a far better plane of existence with Allah Himself. When Āsiyah ﵂ was being tortured to death by Firʿawn, she called out to her Lord, making the following supplication:

رَبِّ ابْنِ لِي عِندَكَ بَيْتًا فِي الْجَنَّةِ

"My Lord! Build me a house in Paradise near You."[107]

Upon reflection, one notes here that Āsiyah ﵂ did not just ask for Paradise. Rather, in her invocation, she asked to be with Allah first. Allah positively responded to her request, just as He always answers the martyrs. For as Allah says in another verse:

وَالشُّهَدَاءُ عِندَ رَبِّهِمْ

"...and the martyrs, [who are] with their Lord..."[108]

But they are not only with Him, for at the same time they are also with one another. It is narrated in a Hadith that the souls of the martyrs are placed in green birds that fly freely through Paradise.[109] They recognise and visit one another, and they eat from its fruits and rest in comfort. Imagine the beautiful scene of the martyrs of Gaza—now freed from their open-air prison—soaring beside the martyrs of Srebrenica. Also picture

107 *al-Taḥrīm*, 66:11.

108 *al-Ḥadīd*, 57:19.

109 *Sunan al-Tirmidhī*, 1641.

the souls of the Uyghur martyrs right now embracing those of their brethren from the Rohingya and the people of Kashmir. Those killed in the Nakba 70 years ago are welcoming those killed in Gaza and the West Bank today in the Eternal Garden. The starved martyrs of Yemen and Sudan are now feasting together in the gardens of Jannah. Imagine the martyrs of Lebanon and Syria meeting those massacred across al-Shām (Levant) a thousand years ago. And think of them gathering with the earliest martyrs of this Ummah: Sumayyah, the first to give her life for Islam, Ḥamzah ibn ʿAbd al-Muṭṭalib ﷺ, the Lion of Allah, and Jaʿfar al-Ṭayyār ﷺ, the standard-bearer of the Muslim side in the Battle of Mu'tah. These individuals hold an esteemed status in the sight of Allah. They are called *shuhadā'* (lit. witnesses) not only because Allah witnesses their sacrifice, but because they immediately witness His reward at the moment of death.

And perhaps you have posed the following question after seeing the images of the torn bodies of the Gazan martyrs: What agony must they have endured? Anticipating this question, the Prophet ﷺ told us something remarkable. He said that the martyr feels no more pain at the time of death than a small prick, just like the sting of a needle. By the time we imagine their pain, Allah has already begun bestowing upon them a reward beyond comprehension. This does not dismiss the very real suffering many endure before death. Some die in a slow and painful fashion. But the moment their soul departs, a sense of comfort envelops them that is so complete and overwhelming that the pain is forgotten.

In addition, while other believers are tested in their graves, the martyrs are spared even from the process of questioning altogether. The Prophet ﷺ said that the flashing of swords above their heads was enough of a trial, and by giving up their lives, they have already proven their sincerity.[110] Thus, while we mourn the martyrs of Gaza, we must also take inspiration from them. For their message to us is clear: "We are alive, we are with our Lord, and we are waiting for you to carry on the moral mission of spreading the one true message of Islam."

But what about the ruthless and merciless *jabbārīn* (tyrants) responsible for the deaths of the innocent? Why does it sometimes appear like they are able to escape all accountability for their crimes in this world? Why do the righteous often leave before their time, while the corrupt seem to live long lives, surrounded by luxury and unchecked power? It is important to note that all of this is part of the divine plan of our Creator. Allah never forgets, and He is never neglectful. The Prophet ﷺ said:

إِنَّ اللَّهَ لَيُمْلِي لِلظَّالِمِ، حَتَّى إِذَا أَخَذَهُ لَمْ يُفْلِتْهُ

"Certainly, Allah gives the oppressor time. But when He seizes him, He does not release him."[111]

From our limited point of view, the tyrants may seem to die peacefully, as they are often surrounded by doctors and servants

110 *Sunan al-Nasā'ī*, 2053.

111 *Ṣaḥīḥ al-Bukhārī*, 4686.

in lavish surroundings when they are on their deathbeds. But what no one observes is the agony of their final moments. Just as the soul of the martyr is taken with ease and honour, the soul of the oppressor is dragged out in torment. The pain that begins in their final breaths is only the start of their eternal punishment. Whereas the grave expands to welcome the *shuhadā'*, it is firmly closed in the case of the *jabbārīn*. The very ones who buried the innocent under rubble are now themselves crushed by the suffocating squeeze of the grave. It is no coincidence that the only explicit mention of the punishment of the grave in the Qur'an is in reference to the greatest tyrant of all time: Fir'awn. For Allah says in Sūrah Ghāfir:

النَّارُ يُعْرَضُونَ عَلَيْهَا غُدُوًّا وَعَشِيًّا ۖ وَيَوْمَ تَقُومُ السَّاعَةُ أَدْخِلُوا آلَ فِرْعَوْنَ أَشَدَّ الْعَذَابِ

"They are exposed to the Fire [in their graves] morning and evening. And on the Day the Hour will be established [it will be said], 'Admit Pharaoh's people (āl Fir'awn) into the harshest punishment [of Hell].'"[112]

While we rise and rest with words of *dhikr* (divine remembrance) in the morning and evening, the oppressors and their allies are being exposed to Hellfire. While we thank Allah for His blessings, we also remember His perfect justice being administered to those who once thought that they were untouchable. The noble Companion Abū Hurayrah ﵁ would say each morning: "The night has passed, and the day has come, and the people of Pharaoh are being shown the Fire." And in

112 *Ghāfir*, 40:46.

the evening, he would say: "The day has passed, and the night has come, and the people of Pharaoh are being shown the Fire."[113] Thus, while it is still painful to witness injustice in this world, one should be mindful that the oppressors are already being punished in the Barzakh, and their torment will only increase with time. Many war criminals have passed during our lifetimes, yet their legacy of tyranny continues. That is why some scholars say that the phrase *āl Fir'awn* applies not only to his contemporaries, but to every tyrant who follows his path: they are from his people.

The *jabbārīn* are the polar contraries of the *shuhadā'*. The martyrs gave their lives for a cause greater than themselves. The tyrants, on the other hand, lived only to inflate their egos and pursue their desires at the cost of countless lives. And Allah—in His infinite justice—will show them how insignificant they truly are in the next world. The Prophet ﷺ said: "The arrogant and tyrants will be gathered on the Day of Judgment as small ants in the form of men. People will trample upon them due to their disgrace before Allah."[114] While the tyrants once wore crowns in arrogance, the Prophet said that on the Day of Judgment, the *shuhadā'* will wear crowns of honour. Their heads will be adorned with the most beautiful of headwear, as they walk among the people they died defending. And we often say, "It cannot get worse than this," only to witness tyrants outdo themselves with greater acts of cruelty. But know this: the Prophet ﷺ told us that even as the oppressors are

113 Ibn Rajab al-Ḥanbalī, *Ahwāl al-Qubūr wa Aḥwāl Ahlihā ilā al-Nushūr*, 127.
114 *al-Tawāḍu' wal-Khumūl* 224

being punished in the Barzakh, they are begging for the Day of Judgment to be delayed; this is not because they long for redemption, but because they know that the full punishment of Hell is still to come. The final moment on the Day of Judgement will be momentous. The Prophet ﷺ said that Allah, Whose divine name is al-Jabbār (the Compeller), will seize the heavens and the earth in His Hand. To demonstrate this point, the Prophet ﷺ opened and closed his hand to show this reality, and then he related that Allah will say:

أَنَا ٱلْجَبَّارُ، أَنَا ٱلْمَلِكُ، أَيْنَ ٱلْجَبَّارُونَ؟ أَيْنَ ٱلْمُتَكَبِّرُونَ

"I am al-Jabbār and I am al-Malik (the King). Where are the tyrants now? Where are the arrogant?"[115]

But what about the real pain we carry on a day-to-day basis due to the suffering that the Muslim world experiences? Undoubtedly, there is a grief that lingers, an emptiness that comes from losing the ones we love, especially in ways that are so brutal, public, and prolonged. The response to this is that there is a divine wisdom in why the *shuhadā'* are granted the right to intercede on behalf of 70 members of their family. Those who endured the anguish of seeing their loved ones torn from them—often in the most horrific ways—are honoured through them. The Prophet ﷺ said: "The martyr will intercede on behalf of 70 of his relatives."[116] Take a moment to reflect and ask yourself: how many of those faces that you have seen on

115 *Sunan Ibn Mājah*, 198.

116 *Sunan Abī Dāwūd*, 2522.

your screens showing the genocide in Gaza are now martyrs? How many families in Gaza do *not* have a *shahīd* among them? There is at least one in nearly every single household. Thus, how vast must the Gaza Strip be in Jannah? Such an upshot may be hard to grasp when the images being broadcast on a daily basis are so gruesome. But just like the people in Sūrah al-Burūj, who were thrown into trenches of fire simply for believing in Allah, their next step was into the gardens of Paradise. In this context, think of the hairdresser of the daughter of Firʿawn, who declared her belief in Allah and was cast into a pit of fire along with her children. Yet the Prophet ﷺ said that on the night of al-Isrā' wa al-Miʿrāj, he smelled her sweet fragrance in the highest heavens.

And just as those oppressed believers were lifted and honoured, those tyrants who lived in luxury now suffer in burning torment. Allah says with respect to the oppressors and tyrants of this world:

إِنَّ الَّذِينَ فَتَنُوا الْمُؤْمِنِينَ وَالْمُؤْمِنَاتِ ثُمَّ لَمْ يَتُوبُوا فَلَهُمْ عَذَابُ جَهَنَّمَ وَلَهُمْ عَذَابُ الْحَرِيقِ

"Those who persecute the believing men and women and then do not repent will certainly suffer the punishment of Hell and the torment of burning."[117]

But there is something crucial that is worthy of internalization: while believing in the reward of our martyrs and the punishment of their murderers gives us spiritual peace, it must not weaken

117 *al-Burūj*, 85:10.

or dilute our pursuit of justice in this world. While there is no doubt that the reward of the oppressed is with Allah, the responsibility to confront oppression, to uplift the downtrodden, and to speak truth to power lies with us. The *jabbārīn* devote their lives to dominating this fleeting world because they have nothing else to look forward to. But we have something infinitely better awaiting us. As such, we say to them with the fullest degree of confidence: "Allah is sufficient for us, and He is the best disposer of affairs."

"...so I may do good in what I left behind." Never! It is only a [useless] appeal they make. And there is a barrier [the Barzakh] behind them until the Day they are resurrected.

AL-MU'MINŪN, 23:100

10

What about the innocent children?

There is a popular saying which states: "The smallest coffins are the heaviest to carry." In other words, nothing weighs as heavily on the soul like the death of a child. For a parent, it is a painful episode of grief that goes beyond the realm of words. After all, how do you bury what felt like your entire world? How do you "move on" when the heart that beat inside you is now lowered into the ground? Even when we are told that they are in a better place, that knowledge does not always soften the pain. We still ask: Where are they now?

What happens to the Palestinian children—numbering in the thousands—who are killed and sent to the Barzakh? How do we come to terms with the brutality that ended their lives and the injustice that brought them there?

Before this most recent chapter of genocide in Gaza, it was the image of 12-year-old Muhammad al-Durrah, murdered in his father's arms, that shook the world in 2000. Before the People of the Ditch were thrown into the blazing fire for believing in the one true God, it was the faith of a young boy that enraged a tyrant. That child was executed in front of his people, where an arrow was fired at his body, thereby sparking a genocide. But his story did not end there. Instead, his soul was raised, and Allah immortalised his story in the Qur'an; as such, his legacy lives on. Remarkably, during the time of Umar ibn al-Khaṭṭāb ﵁, as the Islamic empire grew rapidly, Muslims discovered a grave believed to be that of this boy. When they uncovered it, they found his body untouched by the vicissitudes of time. This was centuries after his death, but his body had not decomposed. And he is not alone with this virtuous trait. How many times have we heard of the *shuhadā'* (martyrs)—from Uḥud to Gaza—whose bodies do not decay, with their sacrifices being preserved by Allah? Ḥamzah, Muṣʿab, and others from the Companions ﵃ remained recognizable many centuries later.

In our time, however, many of these bodies are not just lifeless, but they are torn apart by the most advanced weapons; such weapons are not used against soldiers, but against infants and toddlers. These tragedies are not collateral losses, but they are

Children who die have a unique and honoured station in the Barzakh. Allah, in His infinite mercy, refuses to let their story end in tragedy. Their short lives are not devoid of a divinely-set purpose.

the targets of the brutal and unjust occupation and reflects its political *modus operandi*. As Nelson Mandela once said: "There can be no keener revelation of a society's soul than the way in which it treats its children."[118] So what does it say about our world, when the most vulnerable are killed *en masse*—starved, bombed, and buried under rubble—and the world's systems turn a blind eye? This unjust status quo leaves many people to ask difficult and pressing questions, such as the following: Why would Allah allow such a soul to enter the world, only to leave it so soon in such a brutal fashion? Take the heartbreaking story of Muhammad Abu al-Qumsan, who had just collected the birth certificates of his newborn twins, only to learn that they had already been killed. Imagine how a soul descends from the realm of pre-existence, touches this Earth only briefly, and then returns to its Creator, thereby leaving behind silence, grief, and broken hearts. Can we find light in such darkness? The answer is in the affirmative. The Prophet ﷺ said:

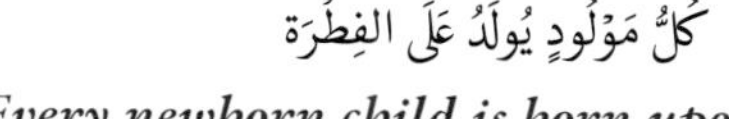

"Every newborn child is born upon the fiṭrah (pure and natural disposition)."[119]

Babies are pure and innocent, but their short lives are not devoid of a divinely-set purpose. Allah, in His infinite mercy, refuses to let their story end in tragedy. We learn from our

118 Nelson Mandela Foundation, "Address by President Nelson Mandela at the launch of the Nelson Mandela Children's Fund, Pretoria," May 8, 1995, http://www.mandela.gov.za/mandela_speeches/1995/950508_nmcf.htm.

119 *Ṣaḥīḥ al-Bukhārī*, 1358.

tradition that children who die have a unique and honoured station in the Barzakh. The Prophet ﷺ once comforted a grieving mother who had lost her son, Ḥārithah, at the Battle of Badr. She asked the Prophet ﷺ, "If he is in Paradise, then I will be patient and seek Allah's reward. But if he is not, I do not know what I will do." The Prophet ﷺ replied:

وَيْحَكِ، أَوَهَبِلْتِ، أَوَجَنَّةٌ وَاحِدَةٌ هِيَ؟ إِنَّهَا جِنَانٌ كَثِيرَةٌ، وَإِنَّهُ لَفِي جَنَّةِ الفِرْدَوْسِ

"Woe to you! Do you think that Paradise is just one level? It consists of many gardens, and he is in the highest level of Jannah al-Firdaws."[120]

Allah thus gave her child more than she could ever give him as a mother. And just like the *shuhadā'*, the souls of these innocent children are placed in the bodies of birds. Ibn Masʿūd ؓ said that the souls of the children of the believers are placed in *ʿaṣāfīr* (sparrows) who fly through Paradise at will and nestle beneath the Throne of Allah. Even the babies who died while they were still nursing are provided care. The Prophet said of his own son, Ibrāhīm, who passed while still nursing: "He has two wet nurses who will complete his term for him in Paradise."[121] Furthermore, Khalid ibn Maʿdān ؒ said that there is a tree in Jannah, Ṭūbā, whose branches are like nursing vessels, and the children of believers are nourished from them.[122] The children of Paradise thus preserve their innocence and pure nature, and their affairs are carefully overseen by the best caretakers imaginable.

120 *Ṣaḥīḥ al-Bukhārī*, 6550.

121 *Ṣaḥīḥ Muslim*, 2316.

122 *Bushra al-Ka'ib*, 67

There is a beautiful vision of the Prophet ﷺ which provides further details regarding the state of the children of Paradise. In it, the Prophet ﷺ said: "I was taken to a lush garden, full of beauty, and in it stood a tall man, so tall that his head touched the sky. Around him were the largest group of children I had ever seen." The Angels who accompanied him explained his vision by stating: "As for the tall man who was in that garden, that was Ibrāhīm ﷺ, and as for the children around him, those are the children who died upon the *fiṭrah*." One Companion asked, "Even the children of disbelievers?" The Prophet said, "Even the children of disbelievers."[123] So humans who leave this world in the age of childhood—regardless of faith or place—are in the care of Ibrāhīm ﷺ and Sārah ﷺ in the next life. In the Hereafter, they are raised by the most patient of souls, namely those who longed for children for decades and were eventually gifted with a nation of Prophets. In the Hereafter, they are given even more, where every innocent soul and every child taken unjustly will now be safe, flying, nurtured, and loved under the care of the greatest souls to ever walk this earth. And one day, their parents will be reunited with them. On that day, there will be no pain, no grief, and no loss. There will only be light, joy, and the eternal company of those little souls we never truly lost.

As we grieve in this world by staring into their empty rooms, clinging to the memories, the toys, and the clothes they once adorned themselves with, we might be tempted to ask about our deceased children: "What does their room in Jannah look

123 *Ṣaḥīḥ al-Bukhārī*, 7047.

like?" Mālik ibn Dīnār ﷺ, a man who once lived far from Allah and drank wine, saw a dream that sparked a paradigm shift in his life. After losing his young daughter, he saw her in a vision with a glowing face, surrounded by silver and gold, and nestled in a cradle of light. She rushed to him, held his hand tightly, and turned back a terrifying beast that was chasing him. Then she climbed into his lap, stroked his beard with her right hand, and recited:

يَا أَبَتِ، أَلَمْ يَأْنِ لِلَّذِينَ آمَنُوا أَنْ تَخْشَعَ قُلُوبُهُمْ لِذِكْرِ اللَّهِ

"O my father! 'Has the time not yet come for believers' hearts to be humbled at the remembrance of Allah?'[124]"

Mālik was shocked to hear this from her, and he began to weep. He said: "Even you, my daughter, know the Qur'an?" She smiled and replied, "We know it even better than you."[125] That story of repentance may have been his, but the station of his daughter is a shared hope for every grieving parent. She is not alone in that mountain of light, and neither are your children. And to the Ummah watching this tragic passage of history unfold and to the parents among us who have suffered this unimaginable grief: know that your children are waiting for you. You could not fully raise them here, but Allah has written a more beautiful story, namely one where they welcome you into the next life.

124 *al-Ḥadīd*, 57:16.

125 Ṣibṭ Ibn al-Jawzī, *Mir'āh al-Zamān fī Tawārīkh al-A'yān*, vol. 11, 426.

He is with you by His knowledge, at every moment of your life. So when you reflect on the audience surrounding your stage, do not forget the most important One watching at all times: Allah.

A man once came to Abū Hurayrah ﷺ and said, "O Abū Hurayrah, I have lost two of my children. Please tell me something from the Prophet that will soothe our hearts from the loss of our loved ones." Abū Hurayrah ﷺ replied by narrating the following Hadith on the authority of the Prophet ﷺ: "Their little ones are the little ones of Paradise. And when one of them meets their parents in the next life, they cling to their garment—just like I am holding the hem of yours—and they will not let go until Allah allows them to enter Paradise together."[126] Your child will grab you by the hand and say, "Not without my parents." Even in the case of a miscarriage, the Prophet ﷺ said that the child will cling to the umbilical cord—the very same cord that may have been torn by the brutality of genocide—and pull their parents into Jannah.

One cannot find any orphans in the Barzakh, since they are all under the care of our father Ibrāhīm ﷺ. But at the same time, it is important to note that there are still orphans *here*, that is, in this temporal world. Our faith places enormous emphasis on caring for them; this is because while Allah has assumed the responsibility of the children whose souls have left their bodies, we are responsible for those whose souls are still alive, but deeply wounded. There are children whose eyes are too familiar with trauma. In addition, there are children whose laughter has been silenced too soon. Moreover, we can find children whose homes are rubble and whose families are shadows. If the sight of shattered bodies disturbs you—as it should—then it behoves

126 *Ṣaḥīḥ Muslim*, 2635.

you to also be disturbed by the shattered spirits of children who live among us today. It is quite likely that those loved ones who have already passed on—such as our sons and daughters, our students, our nieces, and nephews—are watching us now and expecting us to care of the children of this world with compassion. Perhaps at the metaphysical plane of the Barzakh, they are actively asking us: "What are you doing for the ones still left behind?"

"...so I may do good in what I left behind."
Never! It is only a [useless] appeal they make.
And there is a barrier [the Barzakh] behind
them until the Day they are resurrected.

AL-MU'MINŪN, 23:100

11

How to have a bigger grave

You will only truly live in the home you spent your whole life building, and that home is *not* the residence you are decorating now in this temporal world. Rather, it is the one that will greet you after your soul departs your body. Will it welcome you with the warmth of an embrace, or will it tighten with a crushing grip? Will your grave open into a vast garden from the gardens of Paradise, or will it constrict until it feels like your ribs are crushing into one another? Your resting place is not simply situated in a pit that is found six feet under the ground.

It is only as spacious as your virtuous deeds, and as peaceful as your current level of devotion to your Creator ﷻ. That grave—hidden beneath the surface—is either your refuge or your ruin. Imam Ibn Abī Dunyā ؒ narrated that a scholar from the *salaf* (pious predecessors) once said:

لِابْنِ آدَمَ بَيْتَانِ: بَيْتٌ عَلَى وَجْهِ الأَرْضِ، وَبَيْتٌ فِي بَطْنِ الأَرْضِ

"The child of Adam has two homes: one on the surface of the earth, and one beneath it."[127]

And yet paradoxically, most people devote their lives exclusively to the one above the earth. They decorate it, orient it for the four seasons, add doors to the north and south parts of it, and build comfort into every wall. But what about the permanent home that is destined for them below the ground? They leave it barren, forgotten, and crumbling. In light of this reality, a scholar asked a man who was busy beautifying his house, "How long do you expect to live in this home you have built above the surface?" The man replied, "I do not know." Then he asked, "And what about the home beneath the ground: how long will you be in that one?" The man said, "Forever." So the scholar said, "Then should that not be the one for which you prepare?"

Ask yourself this question: Have you built your 'forever home' yet? How solid are its foundations? What spiritual furnishings have you placed inside it? How wide and peaceful is it?

127 Ibn Abī al-Dunyā, *Kitāb al-Qubūr*, 104.

The Prophet ﷺ once led the *janāzah* (funeral) prayer for a man who was born and died in Medina. But he made an unexpected statement: "I wish he had died somewhere other than his birthplace." The Companions asked why he made such a wish. The Prophet ﷺ replied by stating, "Because if someone dies away from the place they were born, a space is measured for them in Paradise as great as the distance from the place he was born to the place where he died."[128] That observation may seem puzzling at first: why would the distance between your birthplace and your deathbed matter? But think about two kinds of people: those who leave home voluntarily for Allah's sake, and those who are forced from their homes by hardship.

Consider the Companions of the Prophet ﷺ and note how many of them died far from their homes: many of them were born in Mecca, yet they died and were buried in Medina. An even more impressive example is the case of Abū Ayyūb al-Anṣārī, a man of Medina, who ended up being buried all the way in the city of Constantinople (modern-day Istanbul). Abū Ayyūb followed the command of Allah and believed in the mission of the Prophet ﷺ so deeply that he pursued it to the edge of the known world. Also, pay consideration to the case of Idrīs, the Prophet who died in the heavens; he ascended in order to ask Allah how much time he had left on Earth so he could plan his *da'wah* (religious call) accordingly. These bright figures are among the elite class that voluntarily left their homes

128 *Sunan al-Nasā'ī*, 1832.

for the sake of Allah. And, in a generous act of reciprocity, Allah accordingly expanded their homes in the next life.

But now reflect on another group: those who did not leave their homes by choice, but instead were forced out. Think of the Palestinian refugee, the Syrian, the Somali, the Uyghur, or the Iraqi, all of whom had keys to their native homes that they can no longer unlock. Their original homes are now reduced to rubble, seized, or sealed off. Some died yearning to return, while others still hold their keys and their dreams close to their hearts. For them, Allah—in His perfect justice—recompenses what was taken. The Qur'an informs us that to be driven from your home is akin to being killed. So, what about those who were displaced and then martyred? To those who were sincere when they left home for Allah's sake, and to those who were patient when driven away by Allah's decree, Allah promises a handsome form of compensation. The ground they were forced to flee from will become their eternal estate. Their graves will be measured not in feet or inches, but in miles, that is, for the vastness of their sacrifice.

But just as Allah's reward is beyond imagination, so too is His punishment beyond comprehension. Suwayd ibn Ghaflah ﵁ narrated a terrifying image of the fate awaiting some in the Hereafter. He said that when Allah wills to abandon the people of Hell, He confines each one in a coffin of fire, sealed with locks of fire, and pierced by pins of fire every time their nerves react in agony. But their ordeal does not end there. That fiery coffin is placed within another, and then enveloped by another casket, with each one being more suffocating than the last, and every one sealed with a lock forged from flame. The process continues until they are buried in layers of fire, kindled on all sides. Each soul presumes that their torment is the worst of all.[129] One can only wonder how dreadful the fate of the tyrants and oppressors who crush and burn the bodies of the innocent will be in this life, but what awaits them is far worse. This is because the grave marks the preview of what a soul will experience in the Hereafter: it is either a luscious plot from the gardens of Jannah, or a pit from the cavities of Hell. That is why when we bury our loved ones, and we lower them into what appears to be a narrow, cold trench, the very first thing we ask from Allah is the following, which is confirmed in a prophetic Hadith:

اللَّهُمَّ اغْفِرْ لَهُ وَارْحَمْهُ، وَعَافِهِ وَاعْفُ عَنْهُ ، وَأَكْرِمْ نُزُلَهُ، وَوَسِّعْ مُدخَلَهُ ، وَاغْسِلْهُ بِالمَاءِ
وَالثَّلْجِ وَالبَرَدِ، وَنَقِّهِ مِنَ الخَطَايَا كَمَا نَقَّيْتَ الثَّوْبَ الأَبْيَضَ مِنَ الدَّنَسِ، وَأَبْدِلْهُ دَارًا خَيْرًا
مِنْ دَارِهِ، وَأَهْلًا خَيْرًا مِنْ أَهْلِهِ، وَزَوْجًا خَيْرًا مِنْ زَوْجِهِ، وَأَدْخِلْهُ الجَنَّةَ وَنَجِّهِ مِنَ النَّارِ

"O Allah, forgive him, have mercy upon him, grant him safety and forgiveness, receive him with honour and make his grave spacious and wash him with water, snow, and hail. And cleanse him from his faults as a white garment is cleaned from its stains. And grant him a home better than his home, a family better than his family, and a mate better than his mate. And enter him into Paradise, protect him from the torment of the grave, and protect him from the torment of the Fire."[130]

129 al-Suyūṭī, *al-Durr al-Manthūr fī al-Tafsīr bi al-Ma'thūr*, vol. 7, 216.

130 *Ṣaḥīḥ Muslim*, 963.

We pray for the new home of our loved ones to be spacious, not just in terms of measurement, but in peace, light, and ease. ʿAwf ibn Mālik ﷺ, who narrated this *duʿā'* (supplication), said that when he heard the Prophet recite it over someone, he sincerely wished he was the one being buried due to how beautiful and powerful the prayer of the Prophet was.

What transpires when a believer is placed in the grave and successfully answers the questions of the two Angels Munkar and Nakīr? They respond by saying, "We knew that you would answer like this." And a voice from the heavens calls out, "My servant has spoken the truth." Immediately thereafter, he is 1) adorned in garments from Paradise, 2) provided furnishings from Paradise, and 3) a gate is opened for him providing him a valuable preview of Jannah. The cool, fragrant breeze of Paradise flows through, and his grave is expanded as far as the eye can see, with one narration saying that it will expand 70 cubits wide. It becomes luminescent like the full Moon. And that, the scholars say, is the baseline perimeter allotted for the believing soul. This is contrasted with the case of the disbeliever, whose grave closes in until his ribs crush together, and a gate to Hell is opened for him. The fire scorches his resting place, and his grave becomes a pit from the pits of Hell.

But here is something even more profound: every grave has a window. If you are destined for Paradise, then you are given a window to Hell, so that you can see what you were saved from such that you can praise Allah for His mercy. And if you are destined for Hell, then you are shown a window to Paradise; such a sight serves as a reminder of what you could have had if you were pious, which becomes a source of endless regret. The grave shows you your home, and your alternative home if you had trekked the opposite path.

When you enter your grave as a believer and see its vastness, light, breeze, and the welcome of the Angels, would you not want to share that moment? Would you not want those you loved to celebrate with you? The answer is obviously in the affirmative. But something unexpected will happen at this juncture. The Prophet ﷺ said:

إِذَا رَأَى الْمُؤْمِنُ مَا فُسِحَ لَهُ فِي قَبْرِهِ، فَيَقُولُ: دَعُونِي أُبَشِّرُ أَهْلِي

"When the believer sees how spacious his grave has become, he will say, 'Let me go back now and tell my family the good news [of my fate].'"

But the Angels will say in response:

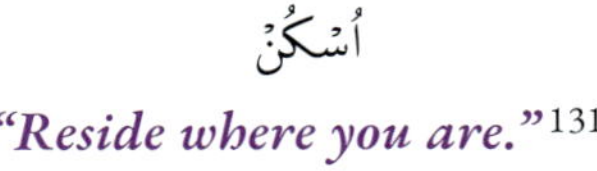

اُسْكُنْ

"Reside where you are."[131]

131 *Musnad Aḥmad*, 14722.

However, there are a multitude of souls in the Barzakh who want to come and see you in your new home and ask about their loved ones. Regarding this momentous event, the Prophet ﷺ said: "The souls of the believers come to him and they rejoice over him more than one of you rejoices when his absent loved one returns." They will begin asking questions, such as the following:

مَاذَا فَعَلَ فُلَانٌ؟ مَاذَا فَعَلَ فُلَانٌ؟

"What happened to so-and-so? What happened to so-and-so?"

And some of them will say:

دَعُوهُ، فَإِنَّهُ كَانَ فِي غَمِّ الدُّنْيَا

"Let him be; he only just recently was relieved from the distress of the world."

The man then asks, "Can I go back and tell my family what I have seen?" But the Angels will say to him:

نَمْ نَوْمَةَ الْعَرُوسِ الَّتِي لَا يُوقِظُهَا إِلَّا أَحَبُّ أَهْلِهَا إِلَيْهَا

"Go to sleep like a newlywed whom none awakens except the most beloved of her family."[132]

132 *Sunan al-Tirmidhī*, 1072.

Imam Ibn Qayyim al-Jawziyyah ﷺ recounts a story about two renowned scholars: Shuʿbah ibn al-Ḥajjāj and Misʿar ibn Kadām ﷺ. He quotes Abū Aḥmad al-Yazīdī ﷺ, who said, "After their deaths, I saw them in a vision, where they were distinguished figures." He said, "I approached Shuʿbah and asked,

مَا فَعَلَ اللَّهُ بِكَ

'What has Allah done with you?'

Shuʿbah ﷺ answered, 'May Allah help you retain what I am about to share with you. My Lord graced me with His love in the gardens of Paradise, beneath a majestic dome. That dome has a thousand entrances crafted from silver and precious stones. Then my Lord addressed me: "O Shuʿbah, you who immersed yourself in the sacred knowledge of Islam, enjoy My nearness. For I am pleased with you."'" He then added that Allah said, "As for My servant Misʿar, who spent his nights in worship and recitation, his reward is to visit Me and gaze upon My noble Face. This is how I reward those who are devout and who refuse to accustom themselves to disobeying Me."[133]

Such is the divine compensation for those who stay true and resist falling into disobedience. The size of your eternal dwelling reflects how much of a priority you made it while living in this *dunyā*. Consider someone who spends their life saving up to build their ideal house in this world: they think about it constantly, visit the site with their family, choose every

---

133 al-Ṣaffārīnī, *al-Buḥūr al-Zākhirah fī 'Ulūm al-Ākhirah*, vol. 1, 320.

detail together, and wait eagerly to move in. Ibn al-Jawzī ﵀ expresses this point beautifully by stating:

لَا دَارَ لِلْمَرْءِ بَعْدَ الْمَوْتِ يَسْكُنُهَا إِلَّا الَّتِي كَانَ قَبْلَ الْمَوْتِ يَبْنِيهَا

"There is no home to live in after death, except the one that was being prepared while they were still alive."[134]

Do not find yourself without a suitable shelter in the Barzakh, because there is no substitute home to move into there. This is why Ibn Maṭṭar ﵀ mentioned that some pious individuals would dig their own graves to stay mindful of death. Contrary to the ultra-materialist vision of the present world order, this *dunyā* is not as substantial as it appears; one of its deceptions is making you believe that it is all there is in terms of reality. In truth, it can suffocate those who fail to see past it. The soul of a believer, however, already feels a vastness even in this life, because it is connected to Allah, to the Angels surrounding us, to the Prophet ﷺ through continuous *ṣalawāt* (salutations), and to the limitless realm of Jannah. That is why, once the soul transitions to the Barzakh, its resting place mirrors and corresponds to that spaciousness. Instead of being confined, it will be expansive.

134 Ibn Abī al-Dunyā, *Kitāb al-Ishrāf fī Manāzil al-Ashrāf*, 171.

12

Now you can fly

Have you ever imagined what it would feel like to fly with wings of your own? Envision yourself being alone with the open sky, being carried by the wind, and free to drift and glide wherever your soul desires. That dream will actually become a reality in the Barzakh. Once the soul is released from the burdens of the physical body, it assumes the form of a bird and begins its journey through a whole new realm, unbound by the limitations of this world. In that space between life and the Hereafter, you are no longer tethered to gravity or struggle to gain altitude. You become a traveller through an unseen world, finally able to soar.

Throughout Islamic history, nearly every renowned scholar has had someone lesser known to thank for shaping them as spiritual leader: they are the quiet teachers whose legacies live on through their students. One such example is Sufyān al-Thawrī ﵀, who used to say that the person who nurtured him the most in his spiritual upbringing was the famous ascetic 'Āmir ibn Qays ﵀. Sufyān would say: "He taught me the Qur'an and so much more."

Sufyān further said, "I used to search for him in his little shop. If I did not find him there, I would go look for him at his home. And whenever I did find him at home, he would be engaged in prayer or reciting the Qur'an with such beauty that it would move the heart. If he was not at home, I would go looking for him in one of the corners of the *masjid* in Kufa, where I would often find him weeping in remembrance of Allah. And if he was not in the *masjid*, he would be at the graveyard crying, reflecting, and holding himself accountable for his deeds." He continued saying: "When 'Āmir ibn Qays passed away, the people of Kufa closed their shops and homes to join his *janāzah*. The entire city came out to bid him farewell." 'Āmir had actually named the great scholar Abū Ḥayyān ﵀ in his will to lead his funeral prayer. Accordingly, as they were carrying his body toward the cemetery, a powerful voice suddenly echoed from the heavens, repeating:

قَدْ جَاءَ الْمُحْسِنُ عَامِرُ بْنُ الْقَيْسِ، قَدْ جَاءَ الْمُحْسِنُ عَامِرُ بْنُ الْقَيْسِ

"The righteous man 'Āmir ibn al-Qays has now arrived! The righteous man 'Āmir ibn al-Qays has now arrived!"[135]

135 *Siyar 'Alam an-Nubala* 6:250

At this point, something incredible happened. A flock of doves appeared overhead that were unlike any birds they had ever seen in terms of number or beauty. In an unprecedented way, these birds were gracefully soaring over his funeral procession. The people stood in awe, overwhelmed by the sight. But Abū Ḥayyān ﷺ turned to them and said, "Do not be astonished. These are the Angels who have come to welcome ʿĀmir back home."[136] That was his funeral reception, but how will ours be when our appointed time to leave this temporal world arrives?

There is something deeply symbolic about birds in our *dīn* (religion). In this *dunyā* (temporal world), the Prophet ﷺ would often use birds as metaphors for how we should live our lives. He would gaze at the sky and draw the attention of the Companions to the birds in flight. Abū Dharr ﷺ said, "The Prophet ﷺ left us, and there was not a single bird that flaps its wings in the sky, except that he gave us knowledge about it."[137] Furthermore, Abū Hurayrah ﷺ narrated that the Prophet ﷺ said:

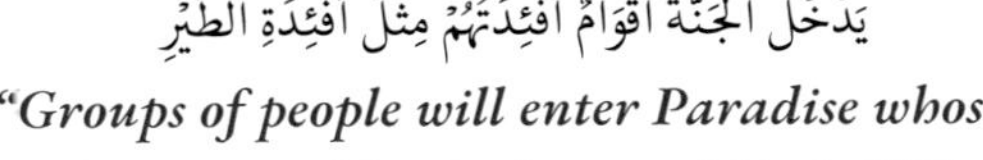

"Groups of people will enter Paradise whose hearts are like the hearts of birds."[138]

136 Ibn al-Jawzi, *al-Muqliq*, 46

137 *Ṣaḥīḥ Ibn Ḥibbān*, 66.

138 *Ṣaḥīḥ Muslim*, 2840.

Imam al-Nawawī ﷺ explained that this is in reference to their *tawakkul* (reliance on Allah) and that birds are also known to have gentle and sensitive hearts.[139] The believers, likewise, are people of softness and reliance on the divine. In regard to that trust, ʿUmar ibn al-Khaṭṭāb ﷺ said that the Prophet ﷺ once remarked: "If you were to trust in Allah with the true trust that is due to Him, He would provide for you just as He provides for the birds. They leave in the morning with empty stomachs, and they return in the evening full."[140] In addition, it is interesting to find that Allah mentions birds as a sign of His *raḥmah* (mercy):

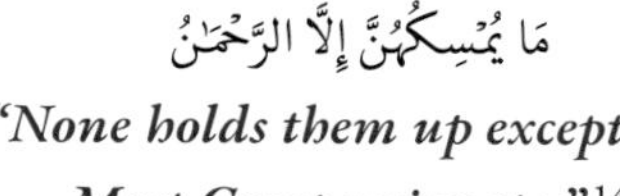

"None holds them up except the Most Compassionate."[141]

Just as birds migrate across lands and through seasons in search of sustenance, in a parallel fashion the believer conducts a journey in pursuit of spiritual nourishment, especially the seeker of knowledge. Ibn al-Qayyim ﷺ beautifully described the believer as a bird. He said: "The body of the bird is the love of Allah, and its two wings are hope and fear." The Prophet also said: "On the Day of Judgment, some believers will pass over the *ṣirāṭ* like birds."[142] May Allah make us among them!

---

139 Al-Nawawi, *al-Minhaaj*, 17:177

140 *Sunan al-Tirmidhī*, 2344.

141 *al-Mulk*, 67:19.

142 *Ṣaḥīḥ Muslim*, 195.

But what about the Barzakh? Imam Ibn al-Qayyim ﵀ said that if you were to examine the connection between souls and bodies, you would realise that the external form reflects the internal spirit. This is to say that every soul assumes a physical form in the Barzakh that mirrors the spiritual image it shaped in the *dunyā*.[143] We know, for instance, that the *shuhadā'* (martyrs) assume the form of beautiful green birds, which are the most stunning of all birds. These birds reside in chandeliers hanging from the Throne of Allah. They have the most beautiful appearance, the best dwelling, and the finest provision. Imam Ibn Kathīr ﵀ said: "As for the souls of the *shuhadā'*, they are in the bodies of green birds, and they are to the rest of the believers like swift riders far ahead on the road."[144] The *shahīd* enjoys a greater level of liberty and spiritual travel because of their ultimate sacrifice for Allah. The souls of children—who died in a pure and innocent state—are also in the form of small, lovely birds with a closeness to the *shuhadā'*. But what about the rest of us? The Prophet ﷺ said:

إِنَّمَا نَسَمَةُ الْمُؤْمِنِ طَيْرٌ يَعْلُقُ فِي شَجَرِ الْجَنَّةِ حَتَّى يَرْجِعَهُ اللَّهُ إِلَى جَسَدِهِ يَوْمَ يَبْعَثُهُ

"The soul of the believer is in the form of a special bird, perching in the trees of Paradise, until Allah returns it to its body on the Day of Resurrection."[145]

143 Ibn al-Qayyim, *Kitab ar-Ruh*, 1:114

144 Ibn Kathir, *Tafsir Ibn Kathir*, 2:164

145 *Sunan al-Nasā'ī*, 2073.

Once the soul is released from the burdens of the physical body, it assumes the form of a bird and begins its journey through a whole new realm, unbound by the limitations of this world.

In this context, Imam Ibn al-Qayyim ﷺ draws out a clear distinction: while the souls of the *shuhadā'* roam freely near the Throne of Allah, ordinary believing souls only perch in the branches of Jannah. Their access and station are high and beautiful, but do not reach the level of the *shuhadā'*.[146] Other scholars also drew a striking parallel: just as earthly birds build their nests in trees and beneath structures, the birds that house the souls of the believers nest under the trees of Paradise. Meanwhile, the birds of the martyrs hover directly beneath the Divine Throne. Analysing this disparity, Imam Ibn Rajab ﷺ said: "Even among the birds of Paradise, there are ranks just like there are among the people. Not all birds are the same." Think about the breathtaking diversity of birds in this dunyā with respect to how much they vary in colour, shape, song, and flight. Then, reflect on how much greater the variety and beauty must be in the Barzakh, and even more so in Jannah, with the permission of Allah.

The fundamental point that is being expressed in this chapter is the following: once it enters the Barzakh, your soul can now travel freely to the places your heart used to be attached to. Your soul moves in the direction of your *du'ā'* (supplication), your deeds, and your longing for Allah. Every time you step outside your house for the sake of Allah, remember these two Hadiths.

146 Omar al-Ashqar, *Minor Resurrection*, p. 137

In the first tradition, the Prophet ﷺ said: "Whoever goes to visit someone solely for the sake of Allah, a voice from the heavens proclaims:

طِبْتَ وَطَابَ مَمْشَاكَ، وَتَبَوَّأْتَ مِنَ الْجَنَّةِ مَنْزِلًا

'You have done well, and your path is blessed; now take your place in Paradise.'"[147]

And with respect to the *shahīd*, the Prophet ﷺ said: "Allah has guaranteed that whoever leaves his home, striving for His cause and affirming the truth of His word, will either be admitted into Jannah, or returned to his home with the reward of Jannah and the blessings of the *dunyā*."[148] Reflect on how this prophetic narration connects to the Barzakh. You step outside in this world to seek sustenance, and in the next realm, your soul returns to its resting place each night with the fruits of that effort. You are—without even realising it—fed from the trees of Jannah that you planted with your good deeds in the *dunyā*. Imam Ibn al-Qayyim ؒ said that there are a number of levels found in the ʿIlliyyīn, which represents the highest plane of Paradise. And the more righteous a soul is, the more freedom it has to ascend. That is why the Prophets ؑ, who are allotted the highest ranks in the Afterlife, can travel instantly from the loftiest heavens to their graves. As for the souls of other believers, the degree of their altitude depends on their personal station in the sight of Allah.

147 *Sunan al-Tirmidhī*, 2008.

148 *Ṣaḥīḥ al-Bukhārī*, 7457.

But what about the disbeliever? When their soul is violently taken and reaches the lowest of the heavens, it is denied entry to the plane of salvation. The Prophet ﷺ described this dramatic moment and then recited the verse:

إِنَّ الَّذِينَ كَذَّبُوا بِآيَاتِنَا وَاسْتَكْبَرُوا عَنْهَا لَا تُفَتَّحُ لَهُمْ أَبْوَابُ السَّمَاءِ وَلَا يَدْخُلُونَ الْجَنَّةَ حَتَّىٰ يَلِجَ الْجَمَلُ فِي سَمِّ الْخِيَاطِ ۚ وَكَذَٰلِكَ نَجْزِي الْمُجْرِمِينَ

"Surely those who receive our revelations with denial and arrogance, the gates of heaven will not be opened for them, nor will they enter Paradise until a camel passes through the eye of a needle. This is how We reward the wicked."[149]

Their soul is recorded in the lowest register of the Sijjīn, which is the lowest level of the Hellfire, and the gates of the heavens are slammed shut before them. Then, violently, their soul is hurled back into their body. The Prophet ﷺ then recited the following verse:

وَمَنْ يُشْرِكْ بِاللَّهِ فَكَأَنَّمَا خَرَّ مِنَ السَّمَاءِ فَتَخْطَفُهُ الطَّيْرُ أَوْ تَهْوِي بِهِ الرِّيحُ فِي مَكَانٍ سَحِيقٍ

"Whoever associates [others] with Allah is like someone who has fallen from the sky and is either snatched away by birds or swept by the wind to a remote place."[150]

In short, the spiritual reality of the disbeliever in this world mirrors his physical state in the Barzakh. His soul lacks wings; it is not lifted, nor is it free. Instead, he is carried to the abyss of darkness and isolation. His soul is exiled, dragged by forces he

149 *al-A'raf*, 7:40.

150 *al-Ḥajj*, 22:31.

cannot control, because it was never anchored to its Creator ﷻ. Accordingly, ask yourself: how high does my soul ascend now? The answer to this question will hint at the wings that your soul will carry in the next realm. How much love do you hold in your heart for Allah while still encased in this physical body? That love will shape your form and freedom in the Barzakh. Is it not the case that the fruits of your trees in Jannah constitute the yield of your deeds here in this life? You have watered those trees with prayer, grown them with remembrance, and now they will blossom. When you step into the next world, you will see that harvest season has arrived.

"...so I may do good in what I left behind." Never! It is only a [useless] appeal they make. And there is a barrier [the Barzakh] behind them until the Day they are resurrected.

AL-MU'MINŪN, 23:100

13

Did Allah put you on this special list?

Did your name make the list of the people destined for Paradise? Are you among those who passed the real test of this temporal world? Just like how your family might wait anxiously for news after a job interview or an important exam, your loved ones in the Barzakh are eager to find out how the living are faring, that is, whether they succeeded or failed. In this worldly life, people often conceal who they really are, and lines between right and wrong can be blurred. But once you cross into the Barzakh, everything becomes unmistakably clear. However, how do you know if you made it and crossed the spiritual finish line?

In the Barzakh, there are two foundational records: one for the people of Jannah, and one for the people of Jahannam. Each of those registers includes categories and degrees, but the first and most important question is: are you even recorded in the book of the successful? The Prophet ﷺ once came to the Companions, holding two books in his blessed hands. He asked them, "Do you know what these are?" They replied, "No, O Messenger of Allah, unless you tell us." He said, "The one in my right hand is a register from the Lord of the Worlds that contains the names of those who will enter Jannah, along with the names of their fathers and their tribes. This list is complete, down to the final person, such that there are no additions and no omissions." Then he said, "And the one in my left hand is also from the Lord of the Worlds, and it contains the names of those who will enter Hell, along with their fathers and tribes. This list is sealed and final as well." Hearing this, the Companions asked, "O Messenger of Allah, if it is all already decreed, then what is the point of doing good?" The Prophet ﷺ responded, "Stick to righteousness and stay as close to it as you can. A person who is destined for Jannah will eventually carry out actions that align with it, regardless of their past. And a person destined for the Fire will end up doing deeds that lead them there, even if they had moments of righteousness beforehand." He then made a motion of throwing the two books aside and said,

قَدْ فَصَلَ رَبُّكُمْ فِي الْعِبَادِ فَرِيقٌ فِي الْجَنَّةِ وَفَرِيقٌ فِي السَّعِيرِ

"Your Lord has already decided concerning His servants: 'A group will be in Paradise and another in the Blaze.'[151]"[152]

Fāṭimah bint ʿAbd al-Malik ﷺ, the wife of ʿUmar ibn ʿAbd al-ʿAzīz ﷺ, once said that the Qur'anic passage "A group will be in Paradise and another in the Blaze" was the most frightening verse for ʿUmar.[153] We also know that ʿUmar ibn al-Khaṭṭāb ﷺ would approach Ḥudhayfah ibn al-Yamān ﷺ, the keeper of the names of the hypocrites, and ask him with deep concern, "O Ḥudhayfah, am I listed among them?"[154] Now ask yourself with sincerity and full honesty: how can you prepare for that moment when your record will be revealed? What kind of religious model can you hold onto so tightly and so consistently that it becomes your defining legacy?

The Prophet ﷺ mentioned many deeds by which people are documented and categorised by Allah. For example, Angels stand at the entrance of the *masjid* every Jumuʿah with their scrolls in hand, recording the names of those arriving one by one until the imam begins the *khuṭbah* (sermon), at which

151 *al-Shūrā*, 42:7.

152 *Sunan al-Tirmidhī*, 2141.

153 Abu Nu'aym al-Isfahani, *Hilyat al-Awliya*, 5:269

154 Ibn al-Jawzī, *Kitāb al-Mudhish*, 461.

In this worldly life, people often conceal who they really are, and lines between right and wrong can be blurred. But once you cross into the Barzakh, everything becomes unmistakably clear.

point they roll up their scrolls and stop writing. Ask yourself: are you always barely making it in time, or are you someone whose name is always among the first to be recorded? What about the ranks of the people of *al-ṣaff al-awwal* (the first row) in the *masjid*, who hold a special place with Allah? One should aim to become a member of these exclusive groups so that they may attain the pleasure of Allah. In addition, the Prophet ﷺ also said in a beautiful Hadith:

مَنْ قَامَ بِعَشْرِ آيَاتٍ لَمْ يُكْتَبْ مِنَ الغَافِلِينَ، وَمَنْ قَامَ بِمِائَةِ آيَةٍ كُتِبَ مِنَ القَانِتِينَ، وَمَنْ قَامَ بِأَلْفِ آيَةٍ كُتِبَ مِنَ المُقَنْطِرِينَ

"Whoever wakes up and recites ten verses in the night will not be listed among the heedless. Whoever recites a hundred verses will be recorded among the devout. And whoever recites a thousand verses will be listed among those who have accumulated mountains of reward."[155]

So which virtuous group do you fall into? Do you recite enough of Allah's Book on a daily basis to belong to any of these categories? Is it possible that your devotion is reflected in your day-to-day home life? For example, the Prophet ﷺ said, "When a husband and wife wake one another up to pray during the night, they are listed among the male and females who constantly remember Allah."[156]

155 *Sunan Abī Dāwūd*, 1398.

156 *Sunan Abī Dāwūd*, 1451.

Or it may be that your strength lies in generosity. Are you among those whose hands are always open for the sake of Allah, giving quietly and consistently to those in need? Imam Siraj Wahhaj—may Allah preserve him—used to give a powerful example when encouraging people to give charity. He would say, "Tomorrow, the scrolls will be unrolled with the names of those who gave, and I do not want there to be a zero next to mine." That statement was not just about charity, but about carving one's legacy in the Afterlife. This is because in the other world, all our names will appear on some kind of list. The question is: in which one will your name be found?

The lists in the Barzakh become visible at different moments for different people. And to understand how that process unfolds, consider this remarkable narration about our father, Adam ﷺ. The Prophet ﷺ said: "On the night of al-Isrāʾ wa al-Miʿrāj, the skies were opened for me. And as I arrived at the lowest heaven, I looked up and saw Adam." He then said, "He looked exactly the same as when Allah first created him; nothing had changed about him." The Prophet ﷺ described how Adam ﷺ was seated in the middle of the setting, watching the souls pass before him. "When a pleasant soul came by, one that smelled sweet and carried goodness, he would smile and say: 'Record his name among the highest ranks of the blessed.' But when a wicked soul came with a foul odour, he would cry and say: 'Write his name in the registry of the damned, among those imprisoned in the lowest depths.'"[157]

157 Daraqutni, *Atraf al-Ghara'ib*, 2:236

Reflect on this powerful narration for a moment. Reflect on the people of Gaza, for instance, and how many pure souls have risen through the 'Illiyyīn, causing us to weep on Earth but causing our father Adam ﷺ to smile in the heavens. But what about the rest of us? When do we cry or rejoice for one another anymore? The Prophet ﷺ said that when someone dies and reaches the realm of the dead, the other souls gather around him, eager for news, just like how people crowd around a traveller who has returned from a distant land. They ask: "What happened to so-and-so? What became of so-and-so?"[158] And the person replies, in a confused state, "But did they not come here before me?" What is happening in this narration is shocking and striking. Imagine this: your mother passed away ten years ago, your sibling five years ago, and now you have just died. Your family is waiting to greet you in the Barzakh, expecting the one who died in between to have already arrived. But they are not there. This leads to a shocking realization: they were not among the righteous, so they are not in this blessed company. Their souls did not join the gatherings of the believers, and that can only mean one thing: they were taken elsewhere. Both the soul that just arrived and those who had been waiting for him respond with sorrow, saying: "We belong to Allah, and to Him we shall return. He must have gone to the abyss of Hell."

The gathering of the righteous in the Barzakh will still continue if you are missing from it. They will move on without you in

158 al-Suyūṭī, *Jāmiʿ al-Aḥādīth*, 1795.

their celebration of their good state. So ask yourself: are you absent from the righteous gatherings here in this life? Because if you are not part of the *masjid* community now, not sitting in religious study circles, not volunteering in the paths of good, not standing for justice or encouraging what is right and forbidding what is wrong, then how can you expect to be part of the sacred assemblies in the next realm? In the Barzakh, the believers are brought back together, just as they were connected in this world. They reunite, not just as friends and family, but as fellow travellers who shared a common belief in Allah's promise and worked toward the same destination. It mirrors the Day of Judgment, which is interestingly an intentional parallel. After all, this moment is a preview of what is to come: the rejoicing of receiving your book in your right hand, and being in the company of those who celebrate their salvation. And the joy of meeting your loved ones in the Barzakh is twofold: first, because after years—maybe decades—of missing them, you will finally see them again. But it is also because you now know with certainty that both you and they have been spared from the torment of the grave. You have arrived safely at the next checkpoint of the Hereafter.

What makes the people of salvation so special is that although their belief in Allah was unshakable, they never allowed themselves to feel overly confident about their own standing. That constant self-awareness pushed them to keep striving towards the path of good, never feeling safe until the very end. It is in those final moments that the difference between those with *yaqīn* (certainty) and those who lived in *shakk* (uncertainty) becomes undeniable. In the grave, there is a pivotal moment that defines everything. A window opens, not just indicating where you are going, but to the place you are *not* going. And what you are shown on that fateful day depends on the life you lived. The Prophet ﷺ said that when a believer is laid to rest, a window to the Fire is opened first. He sees its torment, its destruction, and then he is told: "Look at what Allah protected you from." Then, a window to Paradise opens, and he sees its beauty, its blissful state, and he is then told: "This is your home instead." Then the Angels will say:

عَلَى الْيَقِينِ كُنْتَ وَعَلَيْهِ مِتَّ، وَعَلَيْهِ تُبْعَثُ إِنْ شَاءَ اللَّهُ

"You lived with conviction, you died with conviction, and if Allah wills, you will rise again with conviction."[159]

But as for the one who lived without clarity or commitment, it is a different scene. When he is asked, "What was your way? Who was the Messenger?" he will be unable to answer, saying that he only said what he heard others say. There was no true belief; it was all just the empty imitation of others. A window to Paradise is shown to him—a place he could have had—and he is told: "This is what you lost." Then the view changes, whereby a window to Hell is opened, and he sees it and hears: "This is your destination. You lived in doubt, you died in doubt, and if Allah wills, you will be raised with doubt." And then his punishment begins.[160]

159 *Sunan Ibn Mājah*, 4268.

160 *Sunan Ibn Mājah*, 4268.

In the Barzakh, the believers are brought back together, just as they were connected in this world. They reunite as fellow travellers who shared a common belief in Allah's promise and worked toward the same destination.

Now ask yourself: what does "missing out" mean to you? In this life, it might mean turning down an invitation, missing a party, an online trend or "fad", or a worldly opportunity. But in the Barzakh, it means looking at Paradise from afar, only to hear that you gave it up for a paltry sum in this temporal world. And nothing will bring you more peace in that moment than the times you resisted temptation, walked away from sin, and chose Allah over this world. The people who used to invite you to waste time, to disobey Allah, and to mock the value of religion will not be remembered fondly then. In fact, you will be grateful for distancing yourself from them. And if you did not, the memory of such past harmful connections will be especially painful. In this context, it is useful to mention the dream of Ibn 'Umar ﷺ. He said that one night, two Angels took him to the gates of Hell, and he observed the faces of people that he recognised, and people who recognised him. And in horror, he began repeating:

أَعُوذُ بِاللَّهِ مِنَ النَّارِ أَعُوذُ بِاللَّهِ مِنَ النَّارِ أَعُوذُ بِاللَّهِ مِنَ النَّارِ

"I seek refuge in Allah from the Fire, I seek refuge in Allah from the Fire, I seek refuge in Allah from the Fire!"[161]

He continued asking Allah for His protection until the Angels turned him around from that dangerous path and led him to Paradise instead. This is a matter of decisive importance that every Muslim must be cognizant of and reflect on: if your grave opens and you are shown the Fire and you see Paradise

161 *Ṣaḥīḥ al-Bukhārī*, 3788.

in the distance, who will you regret not following more? Who were the people that led lives you admired but did not attempt to emulate? Who tried to pull you toward good, but you ignored them? And conversely, who will you recognise among the people who led you astray? The ones whose influence you followed, even when at the subconscious level you knew better? In the Barzakh, you are able to remember and reflect on your past decisions and your life in the temporal world. If you are being punished by the Angels Munkar and Nakīr for thousands of years, you will be regretting your past mistakes and sins for what will feel like an eternity.

But right now, you still have a different kind of window: the window of opportunity. The door of repentance still remains open. The chance to turn back to Allah before your book is sealed and your soul is carried off remains possible as long as you are still alive in this world. And every good deed you do now—every prayer, every supplication, and every moment of sincerity—becomes something waiting for you when your grave is opened.

14

Deeds that save you from Punishment

Sometimes, all it takes is one deed for a paradigm shift to occur in your life. A single action might be what tips the scales towards or against your favour. But what if that deed was something you barely noticed at the time? It could have been a quiet act of mercy that you have long forgotten, or worse, a small act of cruelty you never bothered to correct or rectify. On the Day when every deed matters, it could be one of those forgotten moments that determines your fate. 'Aṭā' ibn Yasār ﷺ said that when a person is placed in their grave and awakens, it is their deeds that come to greet them. One of them strikes the person gently on the thigh, jolting him awake, and then proceeds to say:

أَنَا عَمَلُكَ

"I am your deeds."

In confusion and fear, the person asks, "Where is my family? Where are my children? Where are my people? And where is everything that Allah gave me?" The deeds respond by stating, "You have left all of that behind—your family, your children, your wealth, and your worldly life. The only entity that will stay with you now is me." The person will then cry out in regret and say,

يَا لَيْتَنِي آثَرْتُكَ عَلَى أَهْلِي وَوَلَدِي وَعَشِيرَتِي وَمَا خَوَّلَنِي اللهُ تَعَالَى إِذْ لَمْ يَدْخُلْ مَعِي غَيْرُكَ

"If only I had made you—my deeds—more important than my family, my wealth, and my people. For you are the only one who stayed."[162]

The Prophet ﷺ has informed us that three things follow a person to their grave: 1) their wealth, 2) their family, and 3) their deeds.[163] But two of them always leave. The only one that remains with you, that is, the only companion that you will have in that dark and lonely place, is your actions. In this world, you may have been surrounded by loved ones, supporters, and

162 ʿAbd al-Jabbār al-Khawlānī, *Tārīkh Dārayyā*, 48.

163 *Ṣaḥīḥ al-Bukhārī*, 6514.

wealth. It is true that in the Barzakh, you will still be visited, and perhaps even visit others. But in any case, you actually *live with* your deeds. And when they appear before you, the form they assume already provides you a strong impression of what news they will bring. If your deeds were sincere and righteous, you will see a beautiful figure that brings you comfort. But if your life was steeped in sin, heedlessness, or hypocrisy, what you see will be terrifying. It will reflect what you put forward in the temporal world. That companion, whether beautiful or ugly, is the personification of what you built. Your deeds protect you, accompany you, and in some cases, they even save you.

It is natural to hear about the punishment of the grave and feel overwhelmed, whereby we wonder if we have done enough to attain salvation in the Hereafter. Many feel distant from the high level of piety described in these narrations. But the Prophet ﷺ reminded us that salvation does not only lie in grand and heroic acts. He said: "The most beloved deeds to Allah are those that are done consistently, even if they are small."[164] That means even something as routine as making *wuḍū'* (ritual ablution), if done with sincerity, could lead to washing away the sins that would have otherwise earned a person the punishment in the grave. It is not always the major and momentous deeds that rectify your affair; rather, it is often the small ones done with a sincere heart on a daily basis that improve a person's moral standing. Conversely, many of the punishments in the grave are rooted in depraved habits, that is, sins that become a person's second nature. For instance,

164 *Ṣaḥīḥ al-Bukhārī*, 6464.

gossip, neglecting prayer, and arrogance are all actions done repeatedly without repentance. But just as habits can harm, good habits can protect the soul. The grave can become a means of purification for the believer, a place to be cleansed so they may enter the Hereafter with less misdeeds to answer for. But for others, it is only a preview and a frightening glimpse of what is yet to come. We have all heard the detailed narration of al-Isrā' wal-Mi'rāj, where the Prophet ﷺ was shown the various punishments faced by souls due to specific sins. Each scene was tied to something done repeatedly and normalised in the *dunyā*. These are not just shocking images; they also constitute warnings, so we can take notice before it is too late.

There is a deeply moving narration found in one of the Hadith compilations of Imam al-Ṭabarānī ﵀ which is so vivid and beautiful in its content that Ibn Taymiyyah and Ibn al-Qayyim ﵀ recommended all Muslims to memorise it. In it, the Prophet describes, one by one, the deeds that will come to a person's rescue in the grave. He said, "I saw a man from my Ummah, overwhelmed with thirst, being turned away from every basin of water. Then his fasting in Ramadan came to him, and it quenched his thirst."[165] Try to recall all those hot days of fasting when you longed for just a sip of water, and how satisfying it felt to break the fast at *ifṭār*. Now imagine that first sip in the Barzakh after the loneliness and journey into the grave. That latter moment is sweeter and far more profound, because it is the cumulative reward for all those moments you restrained

165 al-Ṭabarānī, *al-Aḥādīth al-Ṭiwāl*, 39.

yourself for Allah's sake. The scholars say this parallels a deeper spiritual truth that is revealed by evaluating other Hadiths. With respect to Jannah, the Prophet ﷺ said, "Whoever drinks wine in this world and does not repent from it will be deprived of it in the Hereafter."[166] But if you restrained yourself for the sake of Allah, then you will be honoured with what you once withheld. And likewise, if you gave up water for fasting, then water will be gifted to you when no one else can offer it.

The Prophet ﷺ continued his beautiful description of pious deeds found in al-Ṭabarānī's Hadith, saying, "I saw a man from my Ummah surrounded by darkness. He kept approaching circles of the Prophets, but was turned away. This continued until his *ghusl* (ritual bath) came and took him by the hand, and sat him in their company."[167] Something as simple and private as bathing—when done with sincerity and love for the Sunnah—can be elevated to such a degree that it allows you to join the most honoured of gatherings. For some people, taking *ghusl* is an easy and refreshing endeavour. But for others—whether it be due to the weather, health reasons, hardship, or lack of access—it is a difficult process. Yet, they endure it for the sake of purity, and Allah rewards them with ease and dignity in the Hereafter. Then he ﷺ said in the same lengthy Hadith, "I saw a man from my Ummah lost in total darkness, and then his Hajj and 'Umrah came and pulled him into the light."[168] If you have ever been to Hajj or 'Umrah, you know

166 *Ṣaḥīḥ al-Bukhārī*, 5575.

167 al-Ṭabarānī, *al-Aḥādīth al-Ṭiwāl*, 39.

168 al-Ṭabarānī, *al-Aḥādīth al-Ṭiwāl*, 39.

how the physical process in Mecca surrounds you in spiritual radiance. Everything reminds you of Allah: every step, every sight, and even very tear. You see the Ka'bah, drink the blessed water of Zamzam, walk between Ṣafā and Marwah, and gather in 'Arafah. You are immersed in white garments, and stripped of status much like death. It is no wonder then that those very pilgrimages are what come to your aid during any time of darkness in the Barzakh and drag you into light.

In the same Hadith, the Prophet ﷺ said, "I saw a man from my Ummah trying to shield himself from the Fire, and then his *ṣadaqah* (voluntary charity) came and stood as a barrier between him and the flames."[169] Just as your *ṣadaqah* shields others in this life from hunger, poverty, and from despair, it will likewise become your shield in the grave. And then on the Day of Judgment, it becomes your shade when there is no shade save that of Allah. Then the Prophet ﷺ said in the same Hadith, "I saw a man whose every effort to speak to the believers was ignored. But then his *ṣilah al-raḥm* (observance of family ties) came and called out to them, 'This man preserved the sacred bonds that Allah created, so speak to him!'"[170] Subsequently, the believers turned, smiled at him, shook his hand, and welcomed him into their gathering. In this world, it is unfortunate to find that there are many people who abandon their family for their friends. But in the Barzakh, it is your loyalty to family that earns you the friendship and attention of

169 al-Ṭabarānī, *al-Aḥādīth al-Ṭiwāl*, 39.

170 al-Ṭabarānī, *al-Aḥādīth al-Ṭiwāl*, 39.

the righteous believers. The family unit holds an elevated and preeminent status in the Islamic ethos, and the rights of one's blood relatives must always be observed.

Then the Prophet ﷺ said in the Hadith, "I saw a man from my Ummah who was saved from the Angels of punishment and instead joined the Angels of mercy because of his habit of commanding the good and forbidding the evil."[171] What does it mean to enjoin good and forbid evil? It means you protected the religion by reminding people of the truth when it was easier to stay silent. You stood for the oppressed and challenged the oppressor. And accordingly, it follows that when you are at your most vulnerable state, Allah sends His mercy to protect you the same way you tried to protect His cause. Finally, the Prophet ﷺ said, "I saw a man from my Ummah kneeling behind a curtain, unable to reach Allah, and then his beautiful character came and led him by the hand to the presence of Allah."[172] This is perhaps one of the most profound segments of this beautiful tradition. The Prophet ﷺ, who was the closest one to Allah, said that the people closest to him on the Day of Judgment will be those with the best character.[173] Your manners—your kindness, your patience, and your humility—are not just a social refinement. Rather, they are the very means by which your soul is drawn near to your Lord.

---

171 al-Ṭabarānī, *al-Aḥādīth al-Ṭiwāl*, 39.

172 al-Ṭabarānī, *al-Aḥādīth al-Ṭiwāl*, 39.

173 al-Bukhārī, *al-Adab al-Mufrad*, 272.

The Hadith continues by outlining more vivid scenes, with each showing a deed stepping in as a saviour, light, shield, and a companion. The common theme that ties all these deeds together is that Allah is not only most just, but He is also merciful. He multiplies the good and virtuous acts you performed with sincerity beyond what you can imagine. Even a single sincere act can be enough to tip the scale.

This is the beauty of Allah's mercy: He takes even the smallest deed you do with sincerity and transforms it into something enormous as long as it was performed truly for His sake. But at the same time, we have to be honest with ourselves and deeply reflect on our inward state introspectively. There may be things we need to correct before we reach the grave. Maybe it was a sin we minimised, a person we hurt more than we realised, or a moment of pride, gossip, or injustice for which we have never apologised. There could potentially be a major sin awaiting the intercession of the Prophet ﷺ on our behalf. But whatever it may be, the time to make things right is now. This opportunity to make amends ceases to exist when the grave is sealed and when the window to this world is shut. The pain of repentance and change today is far lighter than the pain of regret in the Barzakh, when there is no more action, but only consequence.

Whatever habit you can build should be fashioned and fortified today. After all, in the end, it may be that one deed—the one you did not think much of—that becomes your salvation. And it would be a tragedy if the sin that drags you down is one you could have easily rectified while you still had the opportunity.

We will not fix what you have ruined

You dug your own grave, and now you are lying in it. Every word that you spoke and every action that you took—or failed to take—are now your only companions in this next stage of existence. Your status here is not decided by your reputation, your wealth, or who you knew. Instead, it is shaped entirely by your deeds: the ones you meant to do well and the ones you failed to rectify. It is easy to underestimate how much weight even the smallest act carries in the other world. A sharp word in anger, a distracted prayer, and a charity given for praise are not just fleeting moments; they are actually measures and yardsticks of your moral standing.

What if the one deed holding you back from salvation is the one you did not think mattered? What if the one that could have saved you is already long forgotten? Imagine a man who robs from a bank, but then gives part of the stolen money to a poor person. Do you think that smile he causes erases his crime? Deeds are not judged only by their outcome, but by how and why they were done. If you were asked to draw your *ṣalāh* (prayer) in the form of a picture, what would it look like? Would it be whole, strong, and beautiful? Or would it appear rushed and malformed such that it is devoid of all its integrals and conditions?

If left unaddressed, deficiencies in your moral state will have spillover effects in the Barzakh as well. Consider the story of Ṭufayl ibn ʿAmr ﷺ, who recounted how a man made Hijrah with him to join the Prophet ﷺ in Medina. But the rough and arid climate made him sick, and over time the illness he developed wore him down. In a moment of despair, he took his own life by cutting his fingers from the joints. His final state was complex and complicated; on the one hand, he was a Muhājir who left his homeland to join the Prophet ﷺ. In an authentic Hadith, the Prophet said those who migrate for Allah have their sins forgiven. But on the other hand, he also lost hope at a critical moment. Ṭufayl later saw this man in a dream. The man appeared in a garden—clearly in a place of mercy—but his hands were wrapped and hidden.

Every word that you spoke and every action that you took–or failed to take–are going to be your only companions in the next stage of existence.

When Ṭufayl ﷺ asked him how his Lord ﷻ treated him, the man replied: "Allah forgave me because of my migration to the Prophet ﷺ." Ṭufayl then asked him why his hands were wrapped and covered. The man said: "I was told:

إِنَّا لَا نُصْلِحُ لَكَ مَا أَفْسَدْتَ

'We will not fix for you what you yourself have ruined.'"

The Barzakh is thus not like Jannah. In Jannah, there is no state of deformity or incompleteness. But in the Barzakh, there are affairs which are left unfinished, because some of our own deeds were left in an incomplete or deficient fashion. Ṭufayl told the Prophet ﷺ about his dream, and almost immediately after hearing this account, the Prophet ﷺ raised his hands in *duʿā'* (supplication) and said:

اَللَّهُمَّ وَلِيَدَيْهِ فَاغْفِرْ، اَللَّهُمَّ وَلِيَدَيْهِ فَاغْفِرْ

"O Allah, forgive his hands. O Allah, forgive his hands."[174]

This report reflects a serious and sobering reality. You can accumulate all the good deeds conceivable in your register, but if you tarnish them with hypocrisy, arrogance, or harm toward others, then you may have undone your own efforts. Even the *shahādah* (testimony of faith) does not guarantee salvation if a person carries a burden of betrayal or injustice. On the Day of Khaybar, some Companions pointed to a man who had died on the battlefield and said, "He is a *shahīd* (martyr)." The Prophet ﷺ swiftly corrected them, saying instead: "No. I saw him in the

174 *Ṣaḥīḥ Muslim*, 116.

Fire because of a cloak he stole from the war booty."[175] He appeared to have done everything in a virtuous and morally consistent fashion, but one sin remained and unaccounted for. Allah warns us of this very pathology in Sūrah al-Ḥujurāt, a Qur'anic chapter that largely pertains to manners and conduct:

يَا أَيُّهَا الَّذِينَ آمَنُوا لَا تَرْفَعُوا أَصْوَاتَكُمْ فَوْقَ صَوْتِ النَّبِيِّ وَلَا تَجْهَرُوا لَهُ بِالْقَوْلِ كَجَهْرِ بَعْضِكُمْ لِبَعْضٍ أَنْ تَحْبَطَ أَعْمَالُكُمْ وَأَنْتُمْ لَا تَشْعُرُونَ

"O believers! Do not raise your voices above the voice of the Prophet, nor speak loudly to him as you do to one another, or your deeds will become void while you are unaware."[176]

This verse relates to the concept of respect, which is a highly ranked matter of character in the Islamic ethos. It explains why many episodes of the punishment in the grave relates to how we treated other people. Even your acts of *ṣadaqah* (voluntary charity) can be invalidated if followed with hurtful reminders or pride. For instance, Allah ﷻ says:

يَا أَيُّهَا الَّذِينَ آمَنُوا لَا تُبْطِلُوا صَدَقَاتِكُمْ بِالْمَنِّ وَالْأَذَىٰ

"O believers! Do not waste your charity with reminders [of your generosity] or hurtful words."[177]

As for fasting and prayer, Abū Hurayrah narrates that the Prophet ﷺ said: "There are those who fast but get nothing from their fast except hunger. And there are those who pray, but

175 *Ṣaḥīḥ Muslim*, 114.

176 *al-Ḥujurāt*, 49:2.

177 *al-Baqarah*, 2:264.

gain nothing from their prayer except a sleepless night."[178] The opposite of this heedlessness is *itqān* (perfection), which refers to doing your deeds with presence and sincerity. Imagine two episodes of *ṣalāh* (prayer) assuming the form of two humans in the Barzakh. One is glowing, radiant, and beautiful, whereby it is made complete with *khushūʿ* (tranquillity), humility, and supplemented with voluntary Sunnah prayers. The other is small, dishevelled, and rushed, a mere and bare *farḍ* (obligatory) prayer with no heart in it. These two will not stand in the same manner, and neither will their reward be of equal value. So strive to perfect your deeds not with quantity, but with sincerity and presence.

Those two human forms in the Barzakh are not going to be equal in terms of size, beauty, or comfort. The one shaped by humility, sincerity, and excellence in worship will reflect all of those foundational values and shine with excellence. The other—neglected, half-formed, and dishevelled—will be exactly what it was in this world: a mere shadow of what it could have been. Thus, we can and should strive to perfect our good deeds, not only for their reward, but so that we can realise their full benefit in our graves and when we meet Allah.

And then, finally, there are the shameless sins, which are enormities that demonstrate no remorse. Such immoral acts are done publicly, or celebrated in the public sphere with pride. In this regard, Imam Ibn al-Qayyim ﵀ relates the informative

---

178 *Sunan Ibn Mājah*, 1690.

story of a man named Shurayḥ ibn ʿĀbid ﷺ. As he was dying, a friend of his, ʿAfīf ibn Ḥārith ﷺ, came to him and said: "O Shurayḥ, if you are able to come to us after death in a dream and inform us of what has happened to you, then please do so." Sometime after Shurayḥ died, he appeared in a dream. ʿAfīf asked him: "Did you not die?" He replied: "Yes, I have." He asked: "How are you?" Shurayḥ replied by saying: "Our Lord has forgiven all of us except for *al-aḥrāḍ*." So he asked him: "Who are the *aḥrāḍ*?" And he answered: "They are the people who others point to when they think of evil."[179] These are the people known by their sins, and their reputations are built on what displeases Allah, and they proudly wore those sins as badges in the *dunyā* (temporal world). We know that the Prophet ﷺ said: "The entirety of my Ummah will be forgiven except those who publicise their sins."[180] So how can someone hope for the best of the Barzakh when they are known for the worst of deeds in the *dunyā*?

Whenever outlining the intricacies of the punishment of the grave, it is imperative to remember that Allah is never unjust. If anything, we are the ones who have wronged ourselves. This point is best reflected by the one the Prophet ﷺ described as being *muflis* (bankrupt) on the Day of Judgment. He will come with mountains of good deeds, such as *ṣalāh*, *ṣawm* (fasting), and *zakāh* (charity). But then, his *mīzān* (scale) is depleted due to the numerous people he harmed with his tongue and limbs. He backbit, slandered, struck others, and unjustly expropriated

179 Ibn Sa'd, *at-Tabaqat*, 7:415

180 *Ṣaḥīḥ al-Bukhārī*, 6069.

the wealth of innocent people. So what does the *muflis* look like in the grave? Their similitude is that of a person who once had a lush, promising garden, but they left it unguarded. They let pests devour the fruit. They did not shield their deeds from the corruption of bad character, oppression, or arrogance. Due to their negligence, that garden metamorphosised into a blazing fire pit.

While the potential of punishment holds true for the wrongdoers, we must always be mindful that Allah's mercy is vast. Every punishment that is mentioned for this category of people is a hypothetical possibility. But the question remains: Do you really want to wait until you enter your grave to see whether you received Allah's mercy or His justice for the deeds you know you were not supposed to be doing? Allah said in the Hadith Qudsī mentioned in the beginning of this chapter, "We will not fix what you yourself have ruined." But He also gave us a gift in this life: the opportunity to mend our faults and oversights before being ensnared by their consequences.

Besides taking the aforementioned points of this chapter into consideration, one final point worthy of mention is that the deeds that one should persistently worry about are the transactional and interpersonal ones that involve other people. A person should be cognizant of the pain that they have caused, the reputations they have damaged, and the rights that they have violated. After all, even a good deed can be eroded and destroyed from the inside by the maladies of arrogance and injustice.

16

Watch your mouth

In one Qur'anic verse, Allah ﷻ cites the golden words of Luqmān ﵀, who states:

إِنَّ أَنكَرَ ٱلْأَصْوَاتِ لَصَوْتُ ٱلْحَمِيرِ

"...the ugliest of all voices is certainly the braying of donkeys." [181]

This verse explains the events embedded in a particularly shocking account. Abū Sulaymān al-Makkī ﵀ narrated how a group of scholars were once passing through a village on their way to Basra. They stopped when they heard a

181 *Luqmān*, 31:19.

strange and painful braying that resembled the sound of a donkey. They asked the people of the town, "What is that noise?" The people answered by stating: "This is the grave of a man who used to yell at his mother. Whenever she spoke to him, he would say: 'Stop braying like a donkey.'"[182] And it so happened that after he died, every night, the sound of a donkey's braying would come from his grave. One cruel repeated word—which he dared to utter to his mother—became his eternal echo. Even uttering the phrase "uff" to one's parents is condemned in the Qur'an, for Allah states:

فَلَا تَقُل لَّهُمَآ أُفٍّ وَلَا تَنْهَرْهُمَا وَقُل لَّهُمَا قَوْلًا كَرِيمًا

"...never say to them [even] 'ugh,' nor yell at them. Rather, address them respectfully."[183]

One could only imagine the fate of those who go beyond simply uttering "uff" by yelling, mocking, insulting, or abusing the very people who raised them. Some of the most cursed people are those who are tyrants at home, especially to their parents. That is why when the Prophet 'Īsā ﷺ spoke from the cradle, one of the first words he stated to those before him was:

وَبَرًّا بِوَالِدَتِي وَلَمْ يَجْعَلْنِي جَبَّارًا شَقِيًّا

"...and [He has bid me] to be kind to my mother. He has not made me arrogant or defiant."[184]

182 Ibn Abī al-Dunyā, *Jāmi' Dhikr al-Qubūr*, 96.

183 *al-Isrā'*, 17:23.

184 *Maryam*, 19:32.

The absence of dutifulness is not neutrality, but pure tyranny. Such a mode of wrongfulness is not just directed against one's parents, however. The tongue can also be used destructively against neighbours, fellow believers, or against anyone who is helpless and unable to defend themselves. A prime example of this is a horrifying story narrated by 'Amr ibn Dīnār ﷺ; he related that the sister of a man in Medina passed away, and she was subsequently buried. When her brother re-entered her grave to retrieve something he accidentally dropped in her burial site, he found a pit of fire where her body lay. Horrified by this sight, he asked his mother about her. She said, "She used to delay her prayers. And she had the bad habit of going to the doors of her neighbours, listening to their conversations, and spreading what she heard."[185] Gossip and eavesdropping all constitute blatant forms of *tajassus* (spying) that are expressly forbidden by Allah in the Qur'an:

وَلَا تَجَسَّسُوا۟

"And do not spy..."[186]

And if that was not enough, there is also the crime of backbiting, a sin that is so detestable that Allah equates it to eating the flesh of one's dead brother. For as Allah also states in the aforementioned verse:

185 Ibn Abī al-Dunyā, *Jāmi' Dhikr al-Qubūr*, 97.

186 *al-Ḥujurāt*, 49:12.

وَلَا يَغْتَب بَّعْضُكُم بَعْضًاۚ أَيُحِبُّ أَحَدُكُمْ أَن يَأْكُلَ لَحْمَ أَخِيهِ مَيْتًا
فَكَرِهْتُمُوهُۚ وَاتَّقُوا اللَّهَۚ إِنَّ اللَّهَ تَوَّابٌ رَّحِيمٌ

"...nor backbite one another. Would any of you like to eat the flesh of their dead brother? You would despise that! And fear Allah. Surely Allah is [the] Accepter of Repentance, Most Merciful."[187]

The Prophet ﷺ once passed by a grave whose occupant was being punishment. He explained this person's dreadful state by saying: "This man used to consume the flesh of the people [i.e. he would backbite his Muslim brethren]."[188] He also described how during his miraculous night journey he witnessed people with nails of copper, scratching their own faces and chests. He asked, "Who are these, O Jibrīl?" And Jibrīl ﷺ replied: "These are those who consumed the flesh of people and violated the honour of others."[189] In another vision, the Prophet saw a man pinned down by one person while a third figure tore his face open with iron hooks on one side, followed by the other. When he asked who this punished individual was, Jibrīl ﷺ answered: "As for the man you came upon, whose sides of mouth, nostrils, and eyes were torn off from front to back, this is the symbol of the man who goes out of his house in the morning and tells so many lies that it spreads all over the world."[190]

---

187 *al-Ḥujurāt*, 49:12.

188 al-Ṭabarānī, *al-Muʿjam al-Awsaṭ*, 2434.

189 *Sunan Abī Dāwūd*, 4878.

190 *Ṣaḥīḥ al-Bukhārī*, 7047.

A Muslim should pause and reflect on the deep warning embedded in these Qur'anic verses and prophetic traditions. Every exaggerated tweet on X, every post on Facebook, every false screenshot, and every casual episode of backbiting carries a serious moral consequence. Every comment, video, or caption that misrepresents, humiliates, mocks, or harms others does not disappear once you die. Rather, it waits for you, and it may just be your companion in the Barzakh. But Allah's mercy is near, even if your tongue has caused harm. The way to undo past transgressions is to control the tongue now, and to sincerely seek forgiveness from those that were wronged. Repent sincerely to Allah, and guard your tongue like it is your heart. The Prophet ﷺ said: "Whoever believes in Allah and the Last Day, let him speak that which is good or remain silent."[191]

On the other hand, the one who guards their tongue, conceals the faults of others instead of exposing them, and remembers Allah often is planting trees in the next world with every utterance of "*subḥānallāh*" (glory be to Allah), "*alḥamdulillāh*" (all praise is due to Allah), "*lā ilāha illa Allāh*" (there is no God but Allah), and "*Allāhu akbar*" (Allah is great) that they recite. The Prophet ﷺ described the souls of the believers to be flying like birds in Paradise, indulging in its luscious and exotic fruits. The trees of Jannah are not watered by rain, but they are actually nourished by remembrance of the divine.

---

191 *Ṣaḥīḥ al-Bukhārī*, 6136.

The key is to habitualise the self with words of light, not darkness. So ask yourself: are you using your tongue to carve out a garden in Barzakh, or to dig a pit of fire? Will you be flying from branch to branch in Paradise, or clawing at your own face because you could not cease speaking ill of others? Be mindful of what leads most people to fall into the Hellfire on the Day of Judgment: the tongue. Likewise, the tongue is what causes many to be punished in the grave. So before your words bury you deeper than your physical deeds ever could, restrain your tongue, and moisten it with the words of *dhikr* (divine remembrance). That way, you will be able to protect the garden that you are going to live in once you depart from this temporal world.

"...so I may do good in what I left behind." Never! It is only a [useless] appeal they make. And there is a barrier [the Barzakh] behind them until the Day they are resurrected.

AL-MU'MINŪN, 23:100

17

Your *wuḍū'* is a serious matter

The smallest acts of today will weigh heaviest on your soul tomorrow. In fact, what seems meaningless today can crush you in the Barzakh. This is not because of the size of the act *per se*, but because of what it uncovers—such as blatant disregard and negligence—towards the One Who commanded you to worship and obey Him alone. Ibn al-Qayyim ﷺ draws a clear connection between law and spirituality by stating that reverence for the law reflects reverence for the Lawgiver.[192]

192 Ibn al-Qayyim, *al-Wābil al-Ṣayyib*, 15.

The way you respond to even the smallest command tells the story of your heart, namely your loyalty, love, and *ta'ẓīm* (reverence) for Allah.

Think about someone you care about, such as a friend, a spouse, or a parent. Sometimes a simple gesture of love, care, or affection can mean the world for them. A speedy check-in, a word of encouragement, and a small but thoughtful gift may appear to be only marginal acts of kindness, but they are arguably infinite in value, as they indicate that one sincerely cares for their loved ones. Conversely, consistently neglecting such acts of beneficence speaks volumes. It is not about failing to contact that relative *per se*, but it is the fact that one did not even think to contact them in the first place.

Extending this same concept to one's relationship with Allah, it can be asked: how can someone who is left unperturbed with filth in a physical or spiritual sense claim love for al-Quddūs (the Pure) and al-Ṭayyib (the Good)? Abū Hurayrah ﷺ once narrated the following chilling Hadith: "We were walking with the Prophet ﷺ; he passed by two graves and paused. Then he said: 'They are being punished, and they are not being punished for something that people think is major. One of them did not take care to keep his garments clean from urine. The other harmed people with his tongue by spreading gossip between them.'"[193] The Companion Abū Bakrah ﷺ reported a similar statement from the Prophet ﷺ, where he

193 *Sunan Ibn Mājah*, 347.

said regarding the two graves: "They are being punished, but not for a sin hard to avoid. As for one, he is being punished for the habit of soiling himself with urine. As for the other, he is being punished for the habit of backbiting."[194] In essence, one lacked care and compassion, while the other lacked restraint. The defining nexus between gossip and negligence in cleanliness is a problematic mindset, where the party in question downplays their misdeed as a trivial matter. Carelessness with speech and carelessness with cleanliness both stem from the same pathology: a heart that does not pay attention, and a soul that relegates Allah's commands to mere proposals. The Prophet ﷺ said: "Most of the punishment in the grave is due to being negligent with urine, so avoid soiling yourself."[195] This is not because it is the worst misdeed, but because it is the most common one. Falling into such acts of wrongdoing stem from apathy and a failure to observe Allah's commands seriously.

Allah loves purity both in a physical and spiritual sense, whereby the body, the tongue, and the inner intention are all cleansed of filth and impurities. Allah says:

إِنَّ اللّٰهَ يُحِبُّ التَّوَّابِينَ وَيُحِبُّ الْمُتَطَهِّرِينَ

"Surely Allah loves those who always turn to Him in repentance and those who purify themselves."[196]

194 *Sunan Ibn Mājah*, 349.

195 *Sunan al-Dāraquṭnī*, 466.

196 *al-Baqarah*, 2:222.

Imam Ibn Rajab ﷺ offered a powerful explanation of this very matter in relation to the Barzakh, noting that the grave is not simply a resting place but a reflection of what lies ahead. It is the first station in the journey of the Hereafter, and whatever happens within it mirrors what is to come, whether reward or punishment. This is just like how on the Day of Judgment, a person will be held accountable for two major categories of rights: 1) *ḥaqq Allāh*, the rights owed to Allah, and 2) *ḥaqq al-'ibād*, the rights owed to fellow human beings.[197] When the Prophet ﷺ cited urine as constituting a cause of punishment in the grave, he was not highlighting a matter of hygiene alone but pointing to a deeper spiritual truth. The failure to purify oneself after urinating reflects negligence toward a divine command and falls under the rights of Allah. On the other hand, backbiting causes direct harm to others, and therefore falls under the rights of Allah's servants. Both actions may seem minor in the eyes of people, yet they are severe in the sight of Allah due to what they indicate about a person's attitude toward responsibility and sanctity. These sins are subtle, and for many, they are committed without a second thought. They are easy to fall into and even easier to brush aside. However, their real danger lies in what they reveal: a lack of mindfulness, a disregard for Allah's commands, and a deficiency in spiritual awareness. When a person speaks carelessly, it is not just their tongue that moves; rather, it is their inner state being exposed. Words are never merely value-free utterances that are free of moral consequences. They can either carry weight with Allah or bring destruction to the speaker.

197 Ibn Rajab al-Ḥanbalī, *Tafsīr Ibn Rajab al-Ḥanbalī*, vol. 2, 361.

The first matter to be judged on the Day of Judgment from the rights due to Allah will be the *ṣalāh* (prayer). And the first matter from the rights of people will be bloodshed, that is, murder. But in the Barzakh, the realm between this world and the next, it is not the ultimate acts that are judged first, but instead their precursors and antecedents. Imam Ibn al-Qayyim ﷺ and others explain that just as *ṣalāh* is central to your relationship with Allah, *ṭahārah* (purification) is its foundation. And just as murder is the ultimate violation of the rights of humans, gossip and slander are its seeds. These are the first things scrutinised in the grave, since they comprise the starting points of virtue and vice respectively.[198]

Thus, be considerate of your *wuḍū'* and perform it with perfection. For on the Day of Judgment, it will shine on your limbs like light. In this world, it removes sins, while in the grave, it protects the person who performed it with diligence. But if a person is careless with *najāsāt* (ritual impurities) when carrying out their religious obligations, there will be dire consequences. In a parallel fashion, consider your tongue: if it is used for remembrance, *du'ā'* (supplication), and prayer, it raises your rank. But if it is used to harm others, especially behind their backs, then it causes you to fall both in this life and in your grave. Think about how the state of purity connects to everything and activates so many acts of worship. *Wuḍū'* gives you access to Allah in prayer. And your words about people in their absence define the purity of your heart toward them.

198 Ibn al-Qayyim, *Kitab ar-Ruḥ*, 1:224

Carelessness with speech and carelessness with cleanliness both stem from the same pathology: a heart that does not pay attention, and a soul that relegates Allah's commands to mere proposals.

Your *ṣalāh* comprises the direct link that you enjoy with your Lord. Your speech about others is your relationship with His creation. If either one of these elements is corrupted, your whole *dīn* (religion) is compromised.

Now, it is essential to not implement these narrations too excessively such that one falls into obsessive doubt or hardship. The Prophet ﷺ emphasised balance and clarity; he ordered us not to let any form of *waswasah* (compulsive whispers) to consume us. If you are unsure whether you broke your *wuḍū'*, assume that you have not. If you do not see any impurity on a certain area, then assume that the site or location is clean. These Hadiths are not meant to paralyze you or instil paranoia; rather, they are meant to awaken and rouse those who are careless and gently urge the heedless to be more careful. The one who uses the restroom and walks away without care, and making no effort to avoid *najāsah* from contaminating their body, is the one being warned. The one who does a rushed *wuḍū'* that barely touches the elbows or ankles is being cautioned.

Someone here might ask, "Is all this really that serious?" The answer is in the affirmative, since carelessness in *wuḍū'* is a sign of carelessness in *ṣalāh*. Likewise, carelessness in backbiting is the doorway to even greater sins like slander, which can destroy entire communities. The Prophet ﷺ once related the affair of a man who was to be flogged in his grave with one hundred lashes. The man pleaded until it was reduced to a single strike, but even that one lash caused his grave to be engulfed in fire. When he asked why, he was told: "You prayed without *wuḍū'*, and you passed by an oppressed person without helping him."[199] This is a profound narration; from it, we infer that not having *wuḍū'* demonstrates a blatant disregard for Allah, and not defending the rights of the oppressed shows disregard for His creation. And most of the time, the "oppressed" in front of us is not someone being beaten in the street; it is someone whose reputation is being tarnished in the midst of a conversation. Thus, strive to maintain a pure disposition in your inward and outward states. Stand in prayer with *ṭahārah*, and stand for others with honour. After all, the one who does not care about a person's dignity will not care about their property, their wealth, or their rights. And the one who neglects the purity of the body and tongue in this world may find themselves defiled and helpless in the grave.

"...so I may do good in what I left behind." Never! It is only a [useless] appeal they make. And there is a barrier [the Barzakh] behind them until the Day they are resurrected.

AL-MU'MINŪN, 23:100

---

199 al-Ṭaḥāwī, *Sharḥ Mushkil al-Āthār*, 3185.

18

Free yourself from *ribā* and debt

Your debts are not written off or dissolved when you die. The soul of the believer can be held back—in a suspended state—until the balance is settled. Thus, it is worth asking whether it is ever logical to gain a material advantage by trampling someone's honour, infringing on their rights, or taking from their property without just cause. You may gain something here, but at what cost in the Barzakh, when Allah ﷻ Himself assumes the responsibility of settling all outstanding debts?

The Prophet ﷺ warned that the worst form of *ribā* (interest) is to attack the reputation of a fellow Muslim without just cause.[200] That kind of harm—even when done casually with the tongue—exposes a deeper disregard for people's rights, just as stealing does. And the same mindset that leads someone to unjustly take another person's wealth often starts with something relatively trivial, such as dishonouring them in the midst of a conversation.

Most unfortunately, we live in a world dominated by predatory financial systems that thrive on exploitation. These systems fuel war, entrench poverty, reward selfishness, and incentivise inhumanity. But in Islam, the prescribed world order is different and predicated on the principles of morality and sustainability. The believer is taught to live within their means, to avoid taking from the world more than they truly need, and never to bury others in debt to satisfy personal greed. The Prophet took the matter of debt with profound seriousness. Muhammad ibn Jaḥsh ؓ narrates that once while they were sitting with the Prophet, he looked toward the sky, placed his palm on his forehead, and said, "*Subḥānallāh* (Glory be to Allah)! A serious matter has been revealed to me." The Companions were silent, afraid to ask what had occurred. The next morning, when Muhammad ibn Jaḥsh ؓ asked what it was, the Prophet ﷺ replied: "By the One in Whose Hand is my soul, if a man were killed in battle for the sake of Allah, then brought back to life, then killed again, and brought back to

200 *Sunan Abī Dāwūd*, 4876.

life again, and then killed again once more, he would not enter Paradise if he still owed a debt, that is, until it was paid off."[201]

That is the gravity of debt: it can prevent a person from entering Paradise—even a martyr—until it is settled and cleared. Another man once came to the Prophet ﷺ and said, "My brother left behind 300 dirhams. Should I distribute them among his children?" The Prophet ﷺ replied, "Your brother is being detained by his debt. Go pay it off." The man did so as he was commanded, and when he returned, he said, "I paid off all of it, except for two dinars that a woman claimed, though she had no proof." The Prophet ﷺ said, "Give it to her, for she is telling the truth."[202]

But what does it exactly mean when we read in these narrations that the soul is suspended? According to Imam al-Suyūṭī ﵀, it means that the soul is detained and prevented from reaching its noble destination.[203] Al-Ḥāfiẓ al-ʿIrāqī ﵀, who was the teacher of Ibn Ḥajar al-ʿAsqalānī ﵀, added that the judgment about whether that soul is ultimately saved or doomed can even be delayed until the debt is settled.[204] This leads to a shocking conclusion: someone's soul can be detained for decades or even until the start of the Day of Judgment over unpaid dues. This is why at a *janāzah* (funeral), it is not a mere formality when a religious leader or the Imam says, "If the deceased owes anyone

---

201 *Sunan al-Nasāʾī*, 4684.

202 *Ibn Majah*, 2433

203 al-Suyūṭī, *Qūṭ al-Mughtadhī ʿalā Jāmiʿ al-Tirmidhī*, vol. 1, p. 326.

204 al-Suyūṭī, *Qūṭ al-Mughtadhī ʿalā Jāmiʿ al-Tirmidhī*, vol. 1, p. 326.

anything, please come forward." It is not a polite gesture, but an urgent request for their account to be cleared before they are buried.

It did not take long for the Companions of the Prophet ﷺ to become aware of the gravity of outstanding debts. In one case, the Prophet ﷺ refused to lead the funeral prayer of someone who owed two dinars. This was until the noble Companion Abū Qatādah ؓ pledged to pay it off. The next day, the Prophet asked him, "Have you paid it off?" Abū Qatādah ؓ said, "Yes." And the Prophet ﷺ responded, "Now his skin has cooled down from the heat of that debt."[205] The Prophet himself constantly sought refuge from debt. 'Ā'ishah ؓ narrated that a *du'ā'* which she heard the Prophet frequently recite was the following:

اللَّهُمَّ إِنِّي أَعُوذُ بِكَ مِنَ الْمَأْثَمِ وَالْمَغْرَمِ

"O Allah, I seek refuge with You from sin and debt."[206]

When someone asked him why he so often asked for protection from debt, the Prophet ﷺ replied: "Because when a man falls into debt, he lies and he breaks his promises." Debt—when not handled with integrity—can slowly chip away at truthfulness, trust, and sincerity. These are all characteristics of the *munāfiq* (hypocrite). This is why scholars like Imam Ibn Ḥajar ؒ emphasise that a believer must live within their means and avoid debt except in cases of genuine need.

---

205 *Musnad Aḥmad*, 14536.

206 *Ṣaḥīḥ al-Bukhārī*, 2397.

As for those who are forced into debt—not because of greed but because of hardship—then our *dīn* (religion) does not abandon them. In fact, Islam encourages helping them with kindness and mercy. The Prophet ﷺ spoke of a man from a previous nation who used to lend to people and tell his servant, "If the debtor is in difficulty, forgive him, so that perhaps Allah will forgive us."[207] And when that man met Allah after passing away, Allah did indeed forgive him. So imagine standing at your grave, weighed down by burdens and regret. But if you had shown mercy to someone in their moment of desperation, perhaps Allah will relieve you in your moment of greatest need.

The other component of the debt equation is far more severe, since it is based on the predatory system of *ribā* (interest). The Prophet ﷺ described its torment in vivid imagery. He said that in a dream, he saw a man swimming in a river of blood, and every time he tried to approach the riverbank, another man would throw a stone into his mouth, forcing him to fall back to where he started. This cycle repeated endlessly. When the Prophet asked Jibrīl ﷺ who the man was, Jibrīl ﷺ replied, "He is the one who used to consume *ribā*."[208] This other-worldly punishment mirrors the very nature of *ribā* itself. Just as the man in life used to trap others in cycles of debt they could never escape from, he is now eternally trapped in a cycle of pain, never reaching relief. Moreover, that stone in his mouth is not just a punishment. Rather, it symbolises how his greed

207 *Ṣaḥīḥ al-Bukhārī*, 3293

208 *Ṣaḥīḥ al-Bukhārī*, 7047.

never ended, even as it harmed others by burdening them with the shackles of interest. The Prophet ﷺ once said that if the son of Adam had a mountain of gold, he would want another; and if given two, he would want a third. He then said: "Nothing will satisfy him until the dirt of his grave enters his mouth."[209] In the case of the one who dealt in *ribā*, it is not just dirt, but a stone, namely a painful symbol of his unquenchable appetite for wealth. The Hadith uses the word *ākil al-ribā* (the consumer of *ribā*). This description is deliberate, as it signifies that the wealth being consumed is not truly that of the charger of interest; in actual reality, it is taken unjustly. And that is true whether a person is charging *ribā* or simply engaging in it willingly by making payments of interest to lenders. Someone from the latter category might object here and say, "But I am not profiting from *ribā*. I am just paying it." But if you participate in a *ribā*-based transaction without necessity or conscience, you are actually helping to sustain the exploitative system and contributing to an economic model that thrives on injustice. This point does not apply to rare and extreme cases where fatwas may allow for concessions due to necessity. Rather, this is regarding those who simply say, "It is what it is. This is how the world works."

Ribā is not just about individual transactions. It is about an exploitative system. It is also about how economies are built to exploit the poor and enrich the powerful oligarchs of the world. Some scholars even interpreted the river of blood in that

209 *Ṣaḥīḥ al-Bukhārī*, 6439.

dream as a metaphor for the violence and chaos that *ribā* causes. Economic injustice feeds political instability, and breeds war, thereby eroding and erasing entire societies. This is why ʿUmar ibn al-Khaṭṭāb ﵁ used to say, "Beware of debt, for it begins with worry and ends in war."[210] We observe this very reality today, as virtually every global conflict has economic interests behind it. If one carefully follows the money trail, they will find someone's greed to be the effective cause of an interstate or intrastate conflict. This is why the one who partakes in *ribā* is told on the Day of Judgment to prepare for war with Allah and His Messenger ﷺ. The Qur'an does not use this language lightly, since it only appears once in the sacred scripture:

فَأْذَنُوا بِحَرْبٍ مِّنَ اللَّهِ وَرَسُولِهِ

"Beware of a war with Allah and His Messenger!"[211]

A person who sold weapons to fuel earthly wars now finds themselves at war with Allah. There can be no fate worse than this. But now compare this exploitative system to *ṣadaqah* (voluntary charity). While *ribā* corrupts and crushes both in a physical and spiritual sense, charity heals and builds in the two realms. It reminds you to live within your means and to be generous, even if you possess little. And it breaks the malady of greed before it adversely affects your Hereafter. One of the most beautiful reminders of this phenomenon comes from a dream that a student had of Imam al-Ghazālī ﵀ after his death.

210 *Muwaṭṭa' Mālik*, 2685.

211 *al-Baqarah*, 2:279.

The student asked, "Which of your many books earned you Allah's mercy?" The Imam replied, "None of them. One night, as I was writing, a fly landed on my ink-pot. I let it drink until it flew away. And Allah forgave me for that."[212] If mercy was written for him over a fly, then what can be said regarding your kindness to a human being in need?

Charity is not given just to help others, but to curb our own desires. It serves as a reminder that we do not need to use *ribā* to gain a few more square feet in this life when we could be expanding our home in the Afterlife. As you resist the temptation to take more in this world, to stretch beyond your means, or to justify entering *ribā* transactions for the sake of worldly comfort, be mindful that every unchecked desire can drag you to somewhere dark. *Ribā* may be a financial affair, but the greed that feeds it, the disregard for others it brings forth, and the war that it invites against Allah and His Messenger ﷺ affects your soul far more than your bank account.

212 al-Ṣanʿānī, *al-Tanwīr Sharḥ al-Jāmiʿ al-Ṣaghīr*, vol. 4, pp. 205-206.

19

The other forms of *zinā*

The unchecked desires of the *nafs* (self) have the power and potency to destroy the soul. *Zinā* (illegal sexual intercourse) is not just a sin; it is a path that leads deeper into darkness, a fire that often begins with a simple glance and ends by consuming everything in its path. Every lustful look and every secret indulgence pulls a person closer to that fire. The question becomes clear: do you choose the cool shade of purity, or the furnace of regret? The Prophet ﷺ once described a terrifying scene he witnessed in a dream. He saw something like a *tannūr* (large oven) that was narrow at the top and wide at the bottom, with fire burning beneath it. Inside it were men and women with no clothing, tormented by flames rising from beneath them. Whenever the fire reached them, they screamed in agony. When the Prophet ﷺ asked the Angels who these people were, they replied, "These are the adulterers from the men and women who are being punished for their acts of *zinā*."[213] While this Hadith specifically refers to those who commit the physical act of *zinā*, it serves as a powerful warning. For those who fall into smaller acts that serve as pathways to *zinā*—such as casual flirting, immodest interactions, and virtual indecency—there may be a lesser but still painful version of this torment in the Barzakh. The slope that leads to *zinā* is steep and slippery, and it is frighteningly easy to fall into it.

There is a consistent theme in the teachings of the Prophet ﷺ regarding *zinā*, where we find that it is often associated with the words heat and fire. In sum, *zinā* begins with the heat of desire; that fire is either fuelled by indulgence or extinguished by the coolness of chastity. The Prophet ﷺ drew a link between chastity and shade, saying that one of the seven categories of people who will be shaded by Allah on the Day of Judgment is the person who resists the temptation of a high-ranking beautiful woman and says, "I fear Allah."[214] At the same time, the Prophet ﷺ described a future time period when maintaining observance of this religion would be like holding a burning coal.[215] Resisting temptation, especially in an age of easy access and constant exposure, requires the patience

---

213 *Ṣaḥīḥ al-Bukhārī*, 7047.

214 *Ṣaḥīḥ al-Bukhārī*, 660.

215 *Sunan al-Tirmidhī*, 2260.

of someone gripping that coal. It is no exaggeration to state that *zinā* is only a few clicks away today, since it can be easily facilitated through phones, computers, and screens of every kind. Many of the punishments in the grave, as described in the Sunnah, relate to lighter manifestations of serious sins. Just like the "dust of *ribā*" touches most people, so too does a portion of *zinā*. Social media, advertisements, billboards, and entertainment all push people toward a lifestyle where *zinā* is not just normalised, but it is glorified. The Prophet ﷺ warned his nation that every human being has a portion of *zinā* that has been decreed for them. It is unfortunately unavoidable in some form: 1) the eyes commit *zinā* through lustful glances; 2) the ears through listening to indecent words; 3) the tongue through inappropriate speech; 4) the hands through unlawful touching; and 5) the feet by walking toward sin.[216] Even if a person does not commit the full act, these steps all pave the way.

In today's world, the virtual form of *zinā* is just as destructive. Watching indecent videos, engaging in obscene conversations, or developing secret online relationships are all manifestations of *zinā*. Interestingly, the Qur'an does not say, "Do not commit *zinā*." Instead, Allah says in one of the clear and decisive verses of His Book:

وَلَا تَقْرَبُوا الزِّنَا إِنَّهُ كَانَ فَاحِشَةً وَسَاءَ سَبِيلًا

"Do not go near zinā. It is truly a shameful deed and an evil way."[217]

216 *Ṣaḥīḥ al-Bukhārī*, 6612.

217 *al-Isrā'*, 17:32.

It is not just an action; it is a lifestyle that strips people of honour and dignity. Additionally, *zinā* lowers the soul while inflaming the most animalistic and lowly of instincts. It is thus no coincidence that the Qur'an often places *zinā* and murder side by side. For instance, in one verse, Allah states:

وَالَّذِينَ لَا يَدْعُونَ مَعَ اللَّهِ إِلَٰهًا آخَرَ وَلَا يَقْتُلُونَ النَّفْسَ الَّتِي حَرَّمَ اللَّهُ إِلَّا بِالْحَقِّ وَلَا يَزْنُونَ

"[The true servants of the Most Compassionate] are those who do not invoke any other god besides Allah, nor take a [human] life—made sacred by Allah—except with [legal] right, nor commit zinā."[218]

Some scholars explain this pairing by saying that murder kills the body, while *zinā* kills the soul. A person consumed by *zinā* may already be spiritually dead before entering the grave. Their passions burn through their relationships, their aspirations, and their peace until it is as if they are already in the *tannūr* described by the Prophet ﷺ. Imam Ibn al-Qayyim ﵀ described the final stage of this addiction as being like a bird that is trapped, unable to free itself.[219] But the journey did not begin with entrapment; rather, it commenced with a glance that was preceded by a moment of heedlessness. A single look, he explains, can be like a poisoned arrow from Shayṭān, striking through the eyes and directly impacting the heart. That is why the Qur'an commands both men and women to lower their gaze.

---

218 *al-Furqān*, 25:68.

219 Ibn al-Qayyim, *al-Jawāb al-Kāfī*, 190.

This is not just for the purpose of modesty, but for attaining spiritual protection. Ibn al-Qayyim ﷺ also notes that when a person lowers their gaze, Allah increases them in light in their heart, their face, and their soul.[220] Perhaps this is why the famous Verse of Light in Sūrah al-Nūr directly comes after the command to guard one's gaze. Those who stay away from the path of *zinā* are rewarded not only with protection in this world but with a brilliant light in the grave and on the Day of Judgment. *Zinā* is not simply about desire, but about trekking toward a dangerous destination. Are you walking toward fire or walking toward light? Are you feeding a desire that will eventually consume you, or are you guarding your soul to keep it radiant and safe?

Imagine the stark difference between the darkness and heat of a grave that has turned into an oven and the brightness and coolness of a grave transformed into a garden. That contrast captures the difference between the path of *zinā* and the pure path of chastity. For those who feel trapped in the darkness of desire and addiction, know this: behind you is a light, and every time you resist temptation, that light grows brighter. This message is not abstract. In actual fact, it is real and true at a personal level.

The addiction to lust and virtual *zinā* is widespread, and its grip can feel unshakable. But you are not alone in your fight. Many are battling the same internal war. Most importantly, Allah

---

220 Ibn al-Qayyim, *al-Jawāb al-Kāfī*, 416.

has not abandoned you. He has not closed the door on His servants. Every time you turn back to Him and every sincere attempt to seek help and break free from this trap is a form of worship. It is a declaration that you would rather lower your head in humility now than endure the burning humiliation of punishment in the grave. Sometimes your room at night feels like your grave, whereby it is dark and isolating. But Allah sees you, and He knows your silent struggles. And from the darkness of disobedience, a path toward *iḥsān*—the station of worshipping Allah as if you can see Him—remains open. Overcoming addiction may expend a significant degree of your energies, but the strength and sincerity you develop in the process may open a door in Paradise that otherwise would have remained closed.

As noted earlier in this chapter, the Prophet ﷺ once said that in times of intense trial and tribulation, holding on to faith will be like holding on to a burning hot coal. That "coal" today often takes the form of a smartphone, an object that gives you instant access to either your destruction or your salvation. If your fear of Allah prevents you from falling into temptation through that screen, then you have chosen something far greater than momentary pleasure, and you have chosen the pleasure of Allah. A powerful story is narrated by al-Suyūṭī about a young man during the time of ʿUmar ibn al-Khaṭṭāb. This young man was known for worshipping regularly in the *masjid*. Every day as he walked to the *masjid*, a woman would call him, inviting him into her home. Her temptation persisted on a daily basis, and for a time, so did his resistance. That was until one day he actually faltered and succumbed to his desire. But as he approached her door, and was about to give in, a verse of the Qur'an came to his heart:

إِنَّ الَّذِينَ اتَّقَوْا إِذَا مَسَّهُمْ طَائِفٌ مِّنَ الشَّيْطَانِ تَذَكَّرُوا فَإِذَا هُم مُّبْصِرُونَ

"Indeed, when Satan whispers to those mindful [of Allah], they remember [their Lord] then they start to see [things] clearly."[221]

As he recited that verse, he collapsed unconscious at her doorstep. When he awoke, he kept repeating the verse until his soul left his body. When news of this event reached 'Umar ﵁, he was heartbroken. He went to console the young man's father, and then he went to the boy's grave and stood over it. With tears in his eyes, he recited:

يَا فَتَى وَلِمَنْ خَافَ مَقَامَ رَبِّهِ جَنَّتَانِ

"O young man, 'And whoever is in awe of standing before their Lord will have two Gardens.'[222]***"***[223]

What this young man unlocked through his fear of Allah, even in that single moment of temptation, was multiple gardens in Paradise. But that fear and state of *taqwā* (God-consciousness) did not come from a moral vacuum. It was cultivated in the *masjid*, in his devotion, and in his connection to the Qur'an.

221 *al-A'rāf*, 7:201.

222 *al-Raḥmān*, 55:46.

223 Jalāl al-Dīn al-Suyūṭī, *Jam' al-Jawāmi'*, vol. 16, 392.

It was his spiritual resilience, built over time, that saved him when he found himself at his weakest state. So ask yourself: What does it feel like to open a *muṣḥaf* and sit quietly in a corner of the *masjid*, letting Allah's words touch your heart? What does it mean to choose to use your phone in private to read Qur'an instead of giving in to fleeting desires? Will you allow the Qur'an to heal and protect you, or will your neglect of it allow temptation to drag you deeper into darkness?

"...so I may do good in what I left behind."
Never! It is only a [useless] appeal they make.
And there is a barrier [the Barzakh] behind
them until the Day they are resurrected.

AL-MU'MINŪN, 23:100

20

When the Qur'an arrives in your grave

The Qur'an will either elevate your soul or crush your entire body; there is no third option or neutral ground. So what are you allowing to fill your mind? For many of us, our mental space is completely depleted, whether in the form of work, chores, children, or school. For others, it is the endless scroll of gossip, entertainment, and mindless information. But here is the definitive truth: what you fill your mind with is shaping your soul. And if the Qur'an is absent, neglected, or treated like background noise, the consequences go far beyond distraction; they could reach into the grave with you. Allah ﷻ said that if the Qur'an were to be revealed upon a mountain, it would shatter in awe of Allah. Yet He made the heart of His Prophet ﷺ able to bear it, and gifted us the same Qur'an to bring life to our hearts. It has the potential to be the spring of our hearts and the light in our chests. But if it is within our heart and its teachings are not internalised, a person's life will be devoid of any blessings. In a Hadith, it is reported that the Prophet ﷺ said:

إِنَّ الَّذِي لَيْسَ فِي جَوْفِهِ شَيْءٌ مِنَ القُرْآنِ كَالبَيْتِ الخَرِبِ

"The one who has no Qur'an in his chest is like a ruined home."[224]

A person without the Qur'an is empty, broken, and forgotten. This is what makes the punishment that the Prophet ﷺ saw in his dream delivered to the neglecter of the Qur'an so petrifying. In the latter account, the Prophet ﷺ described a man lying down while another stood over him with a boulder. Again and again, the second man would crush the first man's skull, and the boulder would roll away. When he returned, the man's head was restored and the punishment was repeated endlessly. When asked what it meant, the Angels told him: "This is the one who learned the Qur'an, but then abandoned it. He neither recites it nor acts upon it, and he sleeps through his prayers at night."[225] This is not about someone who forgets verses due to

224 *Sunan al-Tirmidhī*, 2913.

225 *Ṣaḥīḥ al-Bukhārī*, 7047.

memory loss or age. Rather, it involves a malicious element to it as well in the form of deliberate neglect. The scholars say this is *nisyān* (forgetting) due to *ihmāl* (negligence), a kind of wilful abandonment. Some even said it includes those who learn the Qur'an but then fail to live by its teachings. And that is why the Prophet ﷺ will say on the Day of Judgment:

وَقَالَ ٱلرَّسُولُ يَٰرَبِّ إِنَّ قَوْمِي ٱتَّخَذُواْ هَٰذَا ٱلْقُرْءَانَ مَهْجُورًا

"The Messenger has cried, 'O my Lord! My people have indeed received this Quran with neglect (mahjuran).'"[226]

The word *mahjūr* is a passive participle and is a linguistic cognate of the term *hijrah* (lit. migration), signifying that such people have migrated away from the Qur'an. What could be more heartbreaking than turning away from the very Book that could have saved you? The Qur'an descends like rain, whereby it revives the soft heart and bounces off the hard one. If it is hitting a hardened soul, then ask: Have you closed the door to the one friend that never leaves, that sole companion that wants to guide and protect you?

Some of us fall in love with the Qur'an in Ramadan, but then drift away from it the rest of the year. If that is you, then ask not where the Qur'an has gone, but where *have you gone.* The Sacred Book has been waiting for you, sitting on your shelf, glowing with divine mercy, and ready to be your most loyal companion. It is ready to intercede on your behalf in your grave, and stay with you through your loneliest hours.

---

226 *al-Furqān*, 25:30.

What you fill your mind with is shaping your soul. If the Qur'an is absent, neglected, or treated like background noise, the consequences could reach into the grave with you.

The companions of the Qur'an receive a reward unlike any other, even after death. 'Ubādah ibn al-Ṣāmit ﷺ described what happens to such a person at the moment of death: the Qur'an comes to their side, hovering over them and guarding them from above while they are being washed. It nestles between their chest and their *kafan* (shroud), never leaving them. When they are placed in their grave and questioned by Munkar and Nakīr, the Qur'an comes and says, "By Allah, I will never leave him." Then the Qur'an turns to the soul of the believer and says:

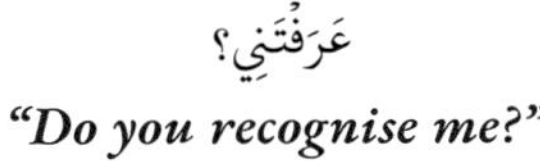

"Do you recognise me?"

And the soul responds, "No, I do not." But the Qur'an replies by stating: "I am your companion, the Qur'an. I kept you awake at night, made you thirsty during the day, kept you away from sin, and restrained your ears and eyes from the forbidden. And today, I will stay with you as a loyal companion." The Qur'an then requests from Allah a mattress from Paradise, a covering, and a soothing incense to fill the grave. A thousand Angels descend with light, perfume, and honour from the heavens, while the Qur'an reclines at your head by the Qiblah, becoming your eternal friend in the Barzakh.[227] All of that will occur if you choose to make the Qur'an a fundamental component of your life, recite it when no one is watching, and let it live in your heart and on your tongue.

---

227 Ibn Ḥajar al-'Asqalānī, *al-Maṭālib al-'Āliyah bi Zawā'id al-Masānīd al-Thamāniyah,* 3500.

The Angels will then gently enter the grave and begin their task of honouring the one who lived with the Qur'an. They place a mattress beneath the deceased's feet, a soft covering beneath his head, and fragrance near his chest. Then they lay him on his right side, in the direction of the Qiblah, and quietly ascend to the heavens. The man will lie there, looking after them, comforted, honoured, and enjoying the company of the best companion imaginable. For near his head, the Qur'an shall be placed, its presence continuing to expand the space of his grave with tranquillity, protection, and light. What was once the most loyal companion in his room, recited by tongue and preserved in heart, is now his companion in the grave, defending him and keeping him company in his solitude. The above mentioned narration applies to the intercession of the entire Qur'an, but within it are special *sūrahs* specifically known for their power to protect a believer from the punishment of the grave. Think of yourself at night, lying down to sleep after a long day, and you take a moment to recite Sūrah al-Mulk before dozing off. The Prophet ﷺ said in a narration reported by 'Abdullāh ibn Mas'ūd ؓ that whoever recites Sūrah al-Mulk every night will be shielded by Allah from the torment of the grave.[228]

However, it is important to note that the Qur'an does not just comprise of words on pages that are read without reflection; its words must be actualised by the heart and embodied by the bodily limbs. 'Uqbah ibn 'Āmir ؓ narrated something powerful

228 *Sunan al-Nasā'ī*, 10547.

reflecting this theme. He reported how the Prophet said that if the Qur'an were written on a skin and then thrown into a fire, it would not burn.[229] How many images have emerged from places of devastation like Gaza, where everything in the vicinity is engulfed in flames, yet the *muṣḥaf* survives? Some scholars interpreted this Hadith to refer to the durable materials the Qur'an was written on in early times, such as bones and leather. But Imam Ibn Qutaybah ﷺ offered a deeper insight in his explanation of this Hadith. He said that it points to a profound reality: "Allah will not let the fire touch a soul that carries the Qur'an."[230] Abū Umāmah ﷺ echoed the same truth, stating: "Recite the Qur'an regularly, memorise it, and live by it. Do not be fooled by the physical copies alone. For Allah does not punish a heart that bears the Qur'an with the Fire."[231]

If you internalise the Qur'an, the Fire of Jahannam cannot consume you because you have already consumed the light of Allah's words. That light becomes your shield, your identity, and ultimately your saviour. Then comes the Day of Judgment, and as you rise from your grave in the state of shock known as al-Fazaʿ al-Akbar (the Great Terror), the Qur'an meets you again. This time, in the form of a pale man, it speaks: "Do you recognise me?" And you say, bewildered, "I do not recognise you." This is because on that day, people forget everything, even their own children and parents. But the Qur'an responds again, stating: "I am your companion, the one who made you

229 *Sunan al-Dārimī*, 3353.

230 Ibn Qutaybah, *Ta'weel Mukhtalif al-Hadith*, 290

231 *Sunan al-Dārimī*, 3224.

thirsty during the scorching days of fasting, the one who kept you awake at night when you could have been asleep. Others profited from their trade [in the temporal world], but today, you will profit from your trade with me." What trade could ever be more profitable than the time you spent with the words of Allah? For every letter, every verse, and every *sūrah* you are raised a degree in Paradise. If you were to stand at the edge of your grave now and look back on your life, how badly would you wish to have made the Qur'an your closest companion? And if you did love and recite it, how much more would you wish to have immersed yourself in its message brimming with the themes of beauty and mercy?

"...so I may do good in what I left behind." Never! It is only a [useless] appeal they make. And there is a barrier [the Barzakh] behind them until the Day they are resurrected.

AL-MU'MINŪN, 23:100

21

The most important prayer of your life

Prayer is not just the wellspring of life in this world, but it is also the source of serenity and security in the metaphysical plane known as the Barzakh after death. Yet in this *dunyā* (temporal world), how many opportunities do we squander and let slip away? You may wake up with 10 minutes before Fajr and resume your sleep for a few more minutes, deciding to forego the opportunity to perform a few *rakʿahs* (units) of *tahajjud* (voluntary night prayers after sleep). You have a few spare minutes before work, but the two *rakʿahs* of Ḍuḥā seem too insignificant to become a steady commitment. The Sunnah units recommended after the obligatory prayers are abandoned for the pull of distractions that barely last a few minutes. Voluntary prayer becomes something we only do when there is absolutely nothing else pressing, and even then, it is usually forgotten. But in the Barzakh, every *rak'ah* becomes priceless. What we so easily overlook here becomes the most coveted gift there.

The Prophet ﷺ informed us exactly what the dead would say if they could communicate. He once passed by a grave and said regarding its occupant:

رَكْعَتَانِ خَفِيفَتَانِ بِمَا تَحْقِرُونَ وَتَنْفِلُونَ يَزِيدُهُمَا هَذَا فِي عَمَلِهِ أَحَبُّ إِلَيْهِ مِنْ بَقِيَّةِ دُنْيَاكُمْ

"Two light rak'ahs, which are belittled and considered as extra (i.e. voluntary) that this person could add to his deeds, are actually more beloved to him than the remainder of your worldly life."[232]

All the wealth, pleasures, and comforts of this *dunyā* as a collective whole cannot compare to two simple units of prayer. What is insightful about this tradition is that the Prophet ﷺ emphasised the performance of light *rak'ahs*, not long nights of *qiyām* (voluntary night prayers). Yet in the next life, those short moments would be priceless in their value. Before Fajr, the Prophet prayed two very short *rak'ahs*. One of the Companions even said it seemed like he only recited Sūrah al-Fātiḥah in both of the units. Despite the brevity of his prayer, the Prophet ﷺ said:

232 Ibn al-Mubārak, *al-Zuhd*, 31.

رَكْعَتَا الفَجْرِ خَيْرٌ مِنَ الدُّنْيَا وَما فِيهَا

"The two rak'ahs of Fajr are better than the entire world and everything within it."[233]

But what is it that prevents us from viewing these acts of worship in the same way? If we explore the stories of the righteous and the friends of Allah, we will be able to find some practical solutions and useful insights. For instance, Imam al-Muzanī ﷺ, the student of Imam al-Shāfiʿī ﷺ, said, "If you want your prayer to benefit you, then say to yourself before each one: 'This might be my last prayer in this life.'"[234] If that thought process guides your heart to the prayer mat, then it is only imaginable what kind of *khushūʿ* (tranquility) would follow.

At the same time, think of your brothers and sisters in Gaza and how they pray between bombs, unsure if they will even live to pray again. In the tents and among the rubble, *ṣalāh* (prayer) becomes not just an obligation but a lifeline. It is not about merely performing a ritual, but about seeking refuge in Allah and attaining tranquility. In times of hardship, prayer becomes the only form of peace that remains. The Prophet ﷺ used to say to the Companion Bilāl ﷺ, who was the *mu'adhdhin* (caller) of the nascent Muslim nation:

---

233 *Ṣaḥīḥ Muslim*, 725.

234 ʿAbd al-Malik ibn Qāsim, *Kitāb wa al-Thaman al-Jannah*, 24.

يَا بِلاَلُ أَقِمِ الصَّلاَةَ، أَرِحْنَا بِهَا

"O Bilāl, give the iqāmah (call for establishing the prayer) for the ṣalāh, so that we may be comforted with it."[235]

This is because for him, prayer was a relief, not a burden. The comfort that a person attains from prayer does not simply exist in this world, but it also extends to the Afterlife. In fact, scholars say that the Prophets still pray in their graves; this is not out of obligation, but because it is more beloved to them than food or drink. When the Messenger of Allah ﷺ passed by the grave of Mūsā ﵇ on the night of al-Isrā' wa al-Mi'rāj, he saw him standing and praying in his grave. As the scholarly commentators noted, this prayer was not increasing his deeds; rather, it was a gift from Allah, and a continuation of the joy and serenity of *ṣalāh*.[236]

Thābit al-Bunānī ﵀ used to make *du'ā'* that Allah would let him pray in his grave. And later, someone did indeed see him in a dream praying in his grave, just as he had hoped.[237] When the believer is resurrected in the grave, the Prophet ﷺ said he will be shown a background scene of where the Sun is about to set. Accordingly, the believer will say:

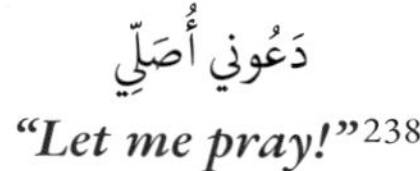

"Let me pray!"[238]

---

235 *Sunan Abī Dāwūd*, 4985.

236 *Sahih Muslim*, 2375

237 Ibn al-Mulaqqin, *Ṭabaqāt al-Awliyā'*, 125.

238 *Sunan Ibn Mājah*, 4272.

He will not ask the Angels who they are or where he is currently situated. Nor will he cry for his wealth or his children. Instead, his heart will cry for the *ṣalāh*. The Angels will say to him: "You will pray, but first you must answer our questions." Even if that believer never missed a *farḍ* prayer, he will still wish he prayed more, especially in the depths of the night. One of the *salaf* said: "I saw Salamah ibn Kuḥayl ﷺ in a dream and asked him: 'What deed did you find most beneficial?' He replied: 'Nothing benefitted me like standing in the night.'"[239] When Mūsā al-Ḥamadānī ﷺ passed away, a relative saw him in a dream with his forehead gleaming like a radiant star. Startled, he asked, "What is this light that I see on your forehead?" Mūsā replied, "That is the light from the dust of my *sujūd* (prostration) on earth." The relative then asked, "And what is your position in the next life?" He answered, "It is the very best. I am in a garden where we will never die and will never be expelled."

As you picture the crowds of believers gathering in the *masjids*, especially during the last ten nights of Ramadan, ponder what their souls might look like in the next world. Kathīr ibn Murrah ﷺ said he once saw himself in a dream entering an elevated place in Jannah. As he walked, amazed by what he saw, he came across a group of women who appeared to be in a *masjid*. He asked, "How did you reach this station?" They replied, "Through our prostration and our proclamations of

239 Ibn Abī al-Dunyā, *al-Manāmāt*, 70.

takbīr (the greatness of Allah)."[240] What do the people of the Barzakh cherish most when they look back at their lives? It is those humble moments, with their heads touching the earth in the solitude of the night. That is what leaves the lasting light in the Hereafter. The Prophet ﷺ taught us that just as a skin that bore the Qur'an will not be consumed by the Fire, the same applies to the place of *sujūd* on your forehead: Allah has forbidden the Fire to touch it. That mark is not a badge of arrogance, nor is it for people to admire. It is the very place through which your soul ascended. It is the sign of your humility before Allah. In your prayer, the moment you are closest to your Lord is in *sujūd*, and the most powerful way to connect with Him is through your *ṣalāh*. But sometimes, the most profound way that Allah draws you closer is not through the means of what you do, but what He puts you through. It is such a trial that humbles you, drives you to the floor, and teaches you to find Him there in the dust. That is the moment where your soul truly begins to rise.

240 Ibn Abī al-Dunyā, *al-Manāmāt*, 91.

22 Why Allah prescribes you bitter medicine

Pain and suffering is an inevitable reality in this life, but you can transform it into something far greater by converting it into your pathway to Jannah. Every one of us will experience grief, loss, and hardship during some stage in this worldly life. And occasionally, the pain becomes so substantial that it feels unbearable. Yet through that very pain, Allah may be carrying you to a place where your deeds alone could never reach. Muṭarrif ibn ʿAbdullāh ﵀ once narrated that on a certain Friday, he and some companions visited the graveyard. As they entered, they saw a deceased person whose funeral procession was in progress; he thought to himself, "Let me take advantage of this opportunity." So, he performed the *janāzah* (funeral) prayer, then stepped just outside the graveyard and prayed two more *rakʿahs* (units); he performed these *rakʿahs* in haste because he was tired. That night, he saw the man from the *janāzah* in a dream. The deceased asked, "Did you just pray two swift *rakʿahs*?" He responded, "Yes." The man replied,

تَعْمَلُونَ وَلَا تَعْلَمُونَ، وَنَحْنُ نَعْلَمُ وَلَا نَسْتَطِيعُ أَنْ نَعمَلَ؛ لَأَنْ أَكُونَ رَكَعْتُ مِثْلَ رَكْعَتَيْكَ أَحَبَّ إِلَيَّ مِنَ الدُّنْيَا بِحَذَافِيرِهَا

"You do deeds without knowing their true value, while we know but can no longer act. To pray like you did—in the form of just two light rakʿahs—is more beloved to me than the entire world and everything in it."

Muṭarrif ﵀ asked, "Who lies in this graveyard?" The man answered, "All Muslims, namely all who did well." Then he asked, "Who is the most virtuous among them?" The man pointed to one grave. In his dream, Muṭarrif made a solemn *duʿā'*, saying:

اَللَّهُمَّ أَخْرِجْهُ إِلَيَّ لِأُكَلِّمَهُ

"O Allah, let him rise and bring him forth before me so I may speak to him."

A young man emerged, unknown to him. Muṭarrif asked, "Are you the most virtuous here?" He said, "That is what they say." Muṭarrif asked, "Was it your *qiyām*, your Hajj, and your jihad that raised you to this rank?" The man said:

قُذِفْتُ فِي الْمَصَائِبِ فَرُزِقْتُ صَبْرًا عَلَيْهَا

"I was thrown into trials, and Allah granted me patience."[241]

That ability to maintain perseverance in the face of tribulation was the fundamental factor that gave him precedence over the rest. Such a finding reflects a simple yet important fact. Sometimes, Allah puts you through hardship not to punish you, but to elevate you instead. And when you pass into the next life, He will show you how He kept His promise.

There is one powerful story that always captures this truth more powerfully than any other, especially when we reflect on the suffering we see today in the Muslim world. Imam al-Awzāʿī ﷺ narrated a fascinating report from ʿAbdullāh ibn Muhammad ﷺ, who was stationed at al-ʿArīsh in Egypt as a patrolman. He came across a tent by the sea, where he found a man with no arms, no legs, and had impaired hearing and vision; the only thing that moved was his tongue. And with that tongue, he was praising Allah, saying: "O Allah, inspire me to praise You with a gratitude worthy of the blessings that You have bestowed upon me, and for the way You have

241 Ibn al-Qayyim, *Kitāb al-Rūḥ*, vol. 1, 19.

favoured me over many of Your creation." 'Abdullāh asked him, "What blessings are you thanking Allah for?" The man replied, "There are some who cannot hear, but I can. Some cannot think, but I can. Some cannot speak, but I can. For that alone, I will keep praising Him." Then he asked 'Abdullāh for a favour. "I had a son who used to help me with *wuḍū'* (ritual ablution), feed me, and give me water. But he has been missing for three days. Could you please look for him on my behalf?" 'Abdullāh went out and found the boy's body in a valley, being devoured by crows. Heartbroken, he said,

إِنَّا لِلَّهِ وَإِنَّا إِلَيْهِ رَاجِعُونَ

"Indeed to Allah we belong and to Him we shall return."

How could he tell the man about this incredible tragedy? He returned to the man and said, "Are you more honourable in the sight of Allah than Ayyūb?" The man said, "No." 'Abdullāh then said: "Then remember what Allah did with Ayyūb: He tested him in his health, his wealth, and his children. And how did He find him? As a patient and grateful person." Then he gently broke the news: "Your son has passed away." The old man said, "Indeed to Allah we belong and to Him we shall return." He weeped profusely, but then he said, "*Alḥamdulillāh* (All praise is due to Allah) that I was not left with a descendant who would disobey Allah." He then continued to cry, which ultimately led to his death a short timespan later.

'Abdullāh covered his body and sat at his head, weeping, waiting for someone to pass. Four men ultimately came by. He told them what had happened. When they saw the man's face, they immediately kissed his eyes and hands. 'Abdullāh became surprised and asked, "Who is this man?" They said, "This is Abū Qilābah al-Jurmī, the companion of Ibn 'Abbās. He was a man that deeply loved Allah and His Messenger ﷺ." Together they washed and shrouded both father and son. They performed the *janāzah* (funeral) prayer and buried them. Later, when 'Abdullāh went to sleep, he saw Abū Qilābah ؒ in a dream, strolling through a garden of Jannah, wearing the garments of Paradise, reciting the verse:

سَلَامٌ عَلَيْكُم بِمَا صَبَرْتُمْ فَنِعْمَ عُقْبَى الدَّارِ

"Peace be upon you for your perseverance. How excellent is the ultimate abode!"[242]

'Abdullāh ؒ asked him, "How did you receive all this?" Abū Qilābah ؒ replied by stating:

إِنَّ فِي الْجَنَّةِ لَدَرَجَاتٍ لَا تُنَالُ إِلَّا بِالصَّبْرِ عِنْدَ الْبَلَاءِ وَالشُّكْرِ عِنْدَ الرَّخَاءِ

"Indeed, there are levels in Jannah that cannot be reached except with patience during trials and gratitude during ease."[243]

242 *al-Ra'd*, 13:24.

243 Ibn Ḥibbān, *Kitāb al-Thiqāt*, vol. 5, 3.

Every hardship you face with beautiful *ṣabr* (patience) is a step closer to what your deeds could not achieve on their own. And every blessing you respond to with *shukr* (gratitude) draws you even higher. Thus, reflect by asking yourself: Have you thanked Allah not just for the joys, but for the trials that shaped you? And have you thanked those people who bore the brunt of your growth, especially those you may have hurt while you were still finding your path to piety?

"…so I may do good in what I left behind." Never! It is only a [useless] appeal they make. And there is a barrier [the Barzakh] behind them until the Day they are resurrected.

***AL-MU'MINŪN*, 23:100**

23

Your loved ones never left you

Our faith teaches us that our deceased loved ones have not truly left us; in actual fact, they are just a station ahead, waiting for our arrival. When someone you love passes away, it can feel like a painful and final separation. But what if the bond between you was never meant to be severed by death? What if there is still a way to remain connected—spiritually, emotionally, and even through prayer? During the time of the Prophet ﷺ, a young man from the Banū Salamah clan named Bishr ibn al-Barā' ؓ passed away, leaving his mother devastated. In her sorrow, she went to the Prophet ﷺ and asked, "O Messenger of Allah, with regard to those from the Banū Salamah tribe who are passing away, can I send greetings to my son Bishr through them?" The Prophet ﷺ comforted her and said, "Yes, indeed! I swear by the One in Whose Hand is my soul, O Umm Bishr, the deceased recognise each other just as birds upon a branch." From then on, every time someone from her tribe was nearing death, Umm Bishr ﵁ would rush to them and say:

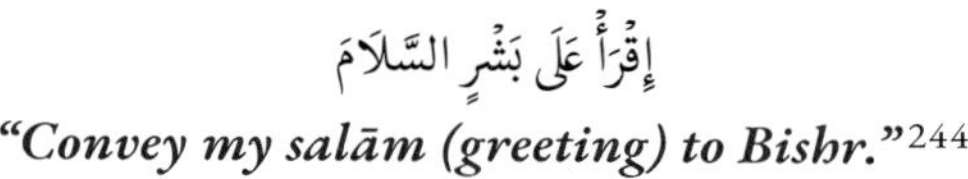

"Convey my salām (greeting) to Bishr."[244]

The following simile is often used as an aid for people mourning their loved ones: think of yourself at a train station. Your loved one has simply boarded earlier, and is just one stop ahead. They do not have phone service anymore, so you cannot speak to them. Nevertheless, they are waiting for you, and the connection—despite being imperceptible—is still very much alive. When your good deeds, especially those of the religion, reach them, they celebrate.

A person's deceased loved ones even wonder who among their living family members got married. Abū Ayyūb ﵁ said: "When the soul of a believer is taken, the other believers welcome him and ask, 'What happened to so-and-so? What happened to

244 Ibn Abi ad-Dunya, *al-Manamat*, 14

so-and-so?' They also ask: 'Did so-and-so get married yet?'" They not only look forward to your arrival there; rather, they still enjoy your visits here. Al-Faḍl ibn Muwaffaq ﷺ, the cousin of Sufyān ibn 'Uyaynah ﷺ, once shared the following account: "When my father passed away, I visited his grave daily. But over time, I started going less. One day, after visiting, I slept and dreamt of him. His grave split open, and I saw him sitting inside, shrouded, bearing the signs of the dead. I began to weep. He looked at me and said:

يَا بُنَيَّ، مَا أَبْطَأَ بِكَ عَنِّي؟

'My son, why have you stopped coming to see me?'

I replied, 'Did you know whenever I would come and visit you?' He said, 'I know every single time. And when you used to come more often, it would comfort me and bring me joy. Even my neighbours in the graveyard felt joy because of your *du'ā'* (supplication).'"[245]

Even if you cannot physically visit your loved one's grave, your *du'ā's* and your deeds done on their behalf are better than any worldly gift you could have provided them while were alive. You were given life in your mother's womb; but after she passes away, you can give life to her grave through *du'ā'*. Your father may have built and furnished your home here, but now you can furnish his home there through your act of *ṣadaqah jāriyah* (continuous charity), your recitation of the Qur'an, or any

245 *Shu'ab al-Iman*, 7525

Whether it is your parents, siblings, children, spouses, or close friends, we all look forward to reuniting with those we loved and cherished, even if we did not get to live with them for long in this world.

virtuous act done for his sake. And if they could speak, that is what they would ask for. ʿĀ'ishah ﷺ said that a man came to the Prophet ﷺ and asked: "My mother passed away, and I believe that if she were alive, should would give charity. Can I do that on her behalf?" The Prophet ﷺ replied, "Yes."[246]

This rule of performing good deeds on behalf of others is not just for your deceased parents. In fact, it is applicable for anyone you loved and lost. Your gifts can reach them before you do. As for those who had no believing family waiting at the next station, they should be pleased to know that they will be welcomed by the best of family, namely the Prophet ﷺ and his Companions, who can be counted among their spiritual kin. What is even more astonishing is that the deceased does get a new family in the Barzakh. One of the authentically transmitted *duʿā's* that the Prophet ﷺ made for the deceased is the following:

وَأَبْدِلْهُ دَارًا خَيْرًا مِنْ دَارِهِ، وَأَهْلًا خَيْرًا مِنْ أَهْلِهِ، وَزَوْجًا خَيْرًا مِنْ زَوْجِهِ

"Replace his home with a better home, his family with a better family, and his spouse with a better spouse."[247]

The famous Hadith commentator Mullā ʿAlī al-Qārī ﷺ explained this prophetic supplication by stating: "The term *ahl* (family) here refers to unique companions in the Barzakh." Others say that it does not mean the individuals are replaced, but that their character is purified, such that there is no more resentment

246 *Ṣaḥīḥ al-Bukhārī*, 2760.

247 *Ṣaḥīḥ Muslim*, 963.

nor bitterness between them; there is only a pure reunion without the difficulties and imperfections of this life. Some scholars say that the report actually incorporates both dimensions, referring to both your old family and the new companions that you will meet in Jannah by the will of Allah.

This ultimately means that your relationship with your loved ones does not end with death. Every *duʿā'*, every prayer, and every act of *ṣadaqah* that you confer and perform in their name is a light that enters their grave. It constitutes a source of comfort and a shimmering proof that love, when rooted in genuine *īmān* (faith), does not end; it actually transcends this world. Whether it is your parents, siblings, children, spouses, or close friends, we all look forward to reuniting with those we loved and cherished, even if we did not get to live with them for long in this world. May Allah reunite us all in Jannah al-Firdaws without any degree of separation, pain, and parting.

24

We will be best friends forever

You have already chosen your companions in the Barzakh, which naturally leads to the next question: who are you walking with now? When the earth draws you within its depths and the soil covers you, it will not just be your family who went ahead that awaits you. The friends you walked with in this life will be your companions in the next. Take a moment and reflect on the following questions: whose faces do you see most? Whose voices are constantly in your ear? Who fills your group chats and lights up your phone? Which part of the Barzakh are they pulling you toward, and which part are you pulling them toward?

In the Barzakh, there is no opportunity to evade the company you chose in this world. You are with those you loved, followed, and walked beside by your volition. Jamīl ibn Murrah ﷺ once said about his beloved friend Muwarriq al-ʿIjlī ﷺ, "He was like a brother to me." One day, Jamīl said to him, "Let us promise one another that whoever among us dies first will visit the other in a dream and tell them what comes after death." Muwarriq agreed with this proposal, and it so happened that he passed away first. Sometime later, Jamīl's wife saw him in a dream. He knocked on their door. She said, "Come in and see Jamīl." But Muwarriq replied, "How can I enter when I have already died?" Then he added, "I only came to tell Jamīl what Allah has done for me, just as we promised. Tell him that Allah has made me from among the *al-muqarrabīn* (those brought near to Allah)."[248]

When it comes to personal relationships, after the beautiful act of *birr al-wālidayn* (dutifulness to parents), no bond is more critical than those initiated and tied for the sake of Allah ﷻ. The Barzakh is the plane where you are reunited with the family that Allah assigned to you, and with the friends you chose. While you did not choose the family you belonged to and your relatives, you did choose your companions. You are in fact currently writing your story in the Barzakh now. Reflect on

248 Ibn Abī al-Dunyā, *al-Manāmāt*, 38.

who is currently within your social circle, such as at home, at work, and even on your screen. Those people will be your company at the Afterlife. The Prophet ﷺ said:

اَلْمَرْءُ مَعَ مَنْ أَحَبَّ

"A person will be with those whom they love."[249]

This prophetic declaration is not limited to righteous scholars or pious friends. It includes celebrities, influencers, and online personalities too. With respect to the individuals you love, follow, and admire, it is imperative to note that you are trekking toward their destiny with them. So reflect on the punishment of the grave, and those whose sins are known to cause them, or those who normalise those sins. If someone is leading you to the path of darkness, remove them now from your social circle, lest you rob yourself of salvation in the Hereafter. The Prophet ﷺ warned:

المَرءُ عَلَى دِينِ خَلِيلِهِ فَلْيَنظُر أَحَدُكُم مَن يُخَالِل

"A person follows the religion of his close friend, so let each of you carefully consider whom he takes as a companion."[250]

Your friends might be Muslim, but are they advising you to be a better and virtuous servant of Allah ﷻ? Do they raise your standards, or lower them? You are either being lifted by your

249 *Ṣaḥīḥ al-Bukhārī*, 6170.

250 *Sunan Abī Dāwūd*, 4833.

companions, or being pulled down by them. Those who gather upon sin, gossip, greed, or heedlessness will find darkness in their graves. But those who came together for Allah's sake by providing aid in the *daʿwah* front, feeding the hungry, seeking knowledge, standing for justice, and encouraging acts of worship will find that the light they built here will illuminate their graves together. That is why the Prophet ﷺ described the strongest bond of faith as not just prayer or charity, but *al-ʿurwah al-wuthqā* (firm grip of faith). Al-Barā' ibn ʿĀzib ؓ narrated that the Prophet ﷺ once asked, "Do you know what the strongest handhold of faith is?" They replied, "The *ṣalāh* (prayer)?" He said:

إِنَّ الصَّلَاةَ حَسَنَةٌ، وَمَا هِيَ بِهَا

"The ṣalāh is definitely excellent, but that is not it."

The Companions named a number of other acts, but in each case, the Prophet ﷺ said that they did not hit the mark with these answers. Eventually, the Prophet ﷺ explained what this extremely virtuous deed is:

إِنَّ أَوْثَقَ عُرَى الْإِيمَانِ أَنْ تُحِبَّ فِي اللهِ وَتُبْغِضَ فِي اللهِ

"The strongest handhold of faith is to love for the sake of Allah and to hate for the sake of Allah."[251]

251 Al-Bayhaqī, *Shuʿayb al-Īmān*, 13.

Those who came together for Allah's sake by providing aid in the da□wah front, feeding the hungry, seeking knowledge, standing for justice, and encouraging acts of worship will find that the light they built here will illuminate their graves together.

The one who truly loves you for the sake of Allah ﷻ will remember you when you depart from this world. They will still be making *du'ā'* for you in your grave, and they will be standing in close proximity to you when we all rise again on the Day of Judgement.

If those who love each other for Allah's sake are placed on pulpits of light on the Day of Judgment, how do you think their graves look like now at the present moment? Do they already meet in the Barzakh? There are some reports from the righteous ascetics of the past which can shed light on this topic. A companion of the scholar 'Āṣim al-Jahdarī ﵀ said, "I saw 'Āṣim in a dream two years after he died. I asked him, 'Are you dead?' He said, 'Yes.' I asked, 'Where are you?' He said: 'By Allah, I am in a garden from the gardens of Paradise, and every Friday morning and evening, I and a group of my companions go to visit Imam al-Muzanī.'" He was then asked, "Do you meet in body or soul?" He replied: "Only the souls gather, for the bodies have decayed."[252]

If a true friend is someone who remembers you in hardship, makes du'ā' for you when you depart from this world, and never leaves you behind, then who better to long for than the Messenger of Allah ﷺ? 'Uthmān ibn 'Affān ﵁, who lived with the Prophet as a leading Companion and friend, was given the most comforting farewell. During the most difficult moment of his life when he was under siege in his own home,

252 Ibn Abī al-Dunyā, *al-Manāmāt*, 58.

fasting, and reciting the Qur'an, he lay down to rest and saw a dream. In it, the Prophet appeared along with Abū Bakr and 'Umar ﷺ. The Prophet ﷺ comforted him and then said:

يَا عُثْمَانُ، أَفْطِرْ عِندَنَا اللَّيْلَةَ

"O 'Uthmān, come and break your fast with us tonight."[253]

Indeed, when 'Uthmān ﷺ woke up, he was assassinated. But he did, in fact, break his fast with the Messenger of Allah in the Barzakh. This beautiful fact requires some pause, since this privilege extends to the believers and does not just apply to the Companions. Over 12,000 people were martyred in Gaza during the Ramadan of 2025 alone. It is very likely that many of them broke their fast with the Prophet ﷺ.

If you knew that the Messenger of Allah ﷺ was waiting for you, who else could you possibly desire to be with? That is why when Bilāl ibn Rabāḥ ﷺ was on his deathbed, his wife was overwhelmed with grief. She stood beside him crying out: "What sorrow! What sorrow!" But Bilāl, with his heart already in the next world, gently corrected her:

بَلْ قُولِي: وَافَرْحَاهْ

"Rather, say: 'What joy!'"

253 Ibn Ḥajar al-'Asqalānī, *al-Maṭālib al-'Āliyah bi Zawā'id al-Masānīd al-Thamāniyah*, 4372.

Then he smiled and said:

غَدًا أَلْقَى الأَحِبَّةَ، مُحَمَّدًا وَحِزْبَه

"Tomorrow, I will meet my beloved ones: Muhammad and his Companions."[254]

It is natural that you and every other Muslim in this world longs for the Prophet ﷺ, and you dream to be in his company. But take a moment to ask yourself whether the people standing next to you today are pulling you closer to him or further away. When you rise on the Day of Judgment, you will be with those you loved and walked with. Thus, imagine standing side by side with the very people who called you to Allah, who lifted your *īmān*, who reminded you to perform the *ṣalāh*, and who helped you purify your soul. Then imagine being greeted by the best of Allah's creation—the Messenger of Allah ﷺ—whereby he recognises you and smiles towards you. He will recognise you as a member of your Ummah. Through good companions, meeting the best of creation becomes a possible endeavour.

254 al-Dhahabī, *Siyar A'lām al-Nubalā'*, vol. 1, 359.

25

People from a past life

You may not be aware of it, but at the metaphysical level you are connected to souls that you have never heard of and to lands you have never visited. How many times have you raised your hands and asked Allah to provide aid to someone that you have never met? Maybe it was done in Ramadan after witnessing a heartbreaking news report in the form of a generic but genuine *duʿā'* (supplication) of, "O Allah, provide aid to the oppressed, cure the sick, and forgive the dead." Furthermore, you may not know them, but what if someone out there is making *duʿā'* for you without even knowing your name?

Du'ā' constitutes as your lifeline and primary connection to Allah. At the same time, it functions as a line that connects hearts across continents, generations, and even realities. It is a link that fuses your soul to the souls of other believers. It is likely that in the Barzakh, you will meet someone that you never saw before, yet paradoxically, you will feel like you have always known them at a deeper level. This is all accounted by the fact that one of you made a *du'ā'* for the other, which created an unbreakable bond. The story of Imam Ibn al-Jawzī ﵀ is telling in this regard. He died on Friday, 12 Ramaḍān 597 AH, and was buried adjacent to the grave of Imam Aḥmad ibn Ḥanbal ﵀.[255] He was blessed by having a wonderful neighbour at his side. And even more beloved than that is the fact that the two first Caliphs of Islam, namely Abū Bakr and 'Umar ﵄, are buried next to the Prophet ﷺ. At their graves, millions pass by them per year and give them words of greeting.

Now, we may not attain the privilege of being buried beside the Prophet ﷺ, but we can still be buried among the righteous, and more importantly, we can be raised with them. 'Abdullāh ibn Nāfiʿ ﵀ said that there was a man who died in Medina and appeared to his companion in a dream, first among the people of Hellfire, and then from the people of Jannah. When asked what caused this change of state, he replied: "There was a righteous man buried with us, and he made *shafā'ah* (intercession) for forty of his neighbours. I was one of them."[256]

255 Ibn Kathīr, *al-Bidāyah wa al-Nihāyah*, vol. 13, 29.

256 Ibn Abī al-Dunyā, *Kitāb al-Qubūr*, 139.

This means that being buried among the believers does benefit the deceased soul.

But such a mode of spiritual ascendance is not just associated with where you are buried. It also relates to who you are bonded with, and what you did for others, even without knowing it. A man once said: "I was traveling and stopped at a masjid for rest. While I was there, the body of a dead person arrived. I did not know the person, but I decided to pray the *janāzah* (funeral) prayer for the reward. Then I followed the body to the cemetery. At the grave, I noticed I was standing alone; the deceased had no family left to stay with him. So I made a *du'ā'*: 'O Lord, this is a guest that has come to You. I do not know him, but if a guest came to me, I would honour him even if I did not know him. So how about You, O Allah, and You are the Most Generous of those who show generosity?'" That night, the man saw a person adorned in white clothes in his dream. The latter asked: "Are you the one who made *du'ā'* for me?" The man asked: "Who are you?" The person in white garments said: "I am the one you buried. And by Allah, Allah forgave me because of your *du'ā'*."

The mercy of Allah is boundless; He has created limitless channels of mercy for the believers in every world, even after death. Just think of how many people have had their funerals arranged in Mecca, Medina, or even your local *masjid*, and the majority of those attending the *janāzah* never even knew them. Yet the Prophet ﷺ said that praying the *janāzah* grants you a mountain of reward like Mount Uḥud, and following the funeral procession doubles the reward. It is important to note that the *du'ā'* we make in the *janāzah* prayer is not limited to one person, for it encompasses every believer:

اللَّهُمَّ اغْفِرْ لِحَيِّنَا وَمَيِّتِنَا

"O Allah, forgive our living and our dead."[257]

And during every Jumu'ah prayer, the imam usually closes their *khuṭbah* (sermon) by making the following *du'ā'*:

اللَّهُمَّ اغْفِرْ لِلْمُؤْمِنِينَ وَالْمُؤْمِنَاتِ، وَالْمُسْلِمِينَ وَالْمُسْلِمَاتِ، الْأَحْيَاءِ مِنْهُمْ وَالْأَمْوَاتِ

"O Allah, forgive the believing men and women, the Muslim men and women, as well as the living among them and the dead."[258]

While it may sound unbelievable, you may be making *du'ā'* for a soul from a thousand years ago. And centuries from now, someone might be making *du'ā'* for you without knowing your name, your story, or your face. This successive and intergenerational chain of *du'ā'*-making is a praiseworthy mode of conduct in our religion. The Prophet ﷺ said: "Whoever seeks forgiveness for the believing men and women, Allah will write for him a good deed for every believing man and woman."[259] In this Ummah, mercy flows both ways, even through the unseen ties of hearts that never met.

---

257 *Sunan Abī Dāwūd*, 3201.

258 al-'Ajlūnī, *Kashf al-Khafā'*, 550.

259 al-Ṭabarānī, *Musnad al-Shāmiyīn*, 2118.

One should not, however, reduce the benefits of these prayers to themselves exclusively. There is an often-overlooked aspect of empathy in our faith. When we see the suffering of our living brothers and sisters around the world, we are spiritually and emotionally moved to make *du'ā'* for them. The Prophet ﷺ said, "The example of the believers in their love, mercy, and compassion for one another is like that of a single body: when one limb is in pain, the rest of the body reacts with sleeplessness and fever."[260]

Now imagine being present at the entrance of a Muslim graveyard. If you could directly observe the suffering of those being punished in their graves—something far more terrifying and painful than the genocide that we see on our current online platforms—what kind of *du'ā'* would you make for them? There is a powerful narration from Bishr ibn Manṣūr ﵀ that is instructive in this regard. He said that there was a man who would regularly attend *janāzah* prayers and visit the graveyard. Each evening, he would stand at the entrance and say: "May Allah ease your loneliness, may Allah have mercy on your isolation, may Allah overlook your sins, and may Allah accept your good deeds." One evening, he was engaged with a number of tasks and was forced to return home without visiting the grave. That night, he saw a large group approaching him in a dream. He asked, "Who are you?" They replied, "We are the people of the graves." He asked, "Why have you come?" They said, "You used to give us a gift before returning home."

---

260 *Ṣaḥīḥ al-Bukhārī*, 6011.

He asked, "What gift?" They replied, "The *du'ā'* you used to make for us every night." He said, "I will resume it." And from that night onward, he never forgot them again.[261]

Ponder on the moment when Bishr passed away and entered the Barzakh. What must it have been like to meet all those souls for which he prayed? Then picture meeting those for whom you made *du'ā'*, namely the people of Gaza, Syria, Sudan, and other lands across the world. Did they feel the warmth of your supplication? What if you could see the effect that your sincere *du'ā'* had on them? Use your words and prayers for good, and you will reap momentous rewards in the Afterlife.

"...so I may do good in what I left behind." Never! It is only a [useless] appeal they make. And there is a barrier [the Barzakh] behind them until the Day they are resurrected.

AL-MU'MINŪN, 23:100

261 al-Bayhaqī, *Shu'ab al-Īmān*, 8860.

26

Your *duʿā'* can change the worlds

Both your *duʿā'* (supplication) and your deeds matter, even when you do not observe their effects. It is likely that you raised your hands in prayer, longing for change, only to discontinue shortly thereafter because the result was not visible. Such a course of action is short-sighted, however. In actual fact, your *duʿā'* was never meant to show you results immediately. Instead, it is quietly shifting realities beyond what you could ever imagine. Perhaps it was your *duʿā'* for Gaza that gave strength to someone's heart, that steadied their feet under the rubble, or even accelerated a future victory. It is possible that your prayer for a loved one changed the course of their life in this temporal world or the Hereafter.

The unseen nature of *du'ā'* does not diminish its power. The world may not move before your eyes, but the very current of fate might be shifting beneath your feet. This is because whenever you make a prayer or a supplication, you are not calling upon a powerless being. Rather, you are calling upon Allah, Who is Rabb al-'Ālamīn (the Lord of all worlds). And your prayer might not just change this world; rather, it could alter someone's world in the Barzakh, or influence events across generations. Maybe someone once prayed for you, and then left this world without ever seeing the consequent impact. And yet, here you are currently present in the world, representing a living testament that their *du'ā'* proved to be effective generations later. In this matter, the example of Sumayyah ﵂, the first martyr in Islam, is instructive. She gave her life with no idea what would unfold through her altruistic and Ummatic sacrifice. It is quite possible that, in the unseen world of the Barzakh, 'Ikrimah ibn Abī Jahl ﵁—a martyr himself and the son of her oppressor—met her after death and said: "It was your patience that helped change everything. After you, Mecca submitted to Allah, and generations followed the path you helped forge."

Through the permission of Allah, it is likely that the martyrs of Gaza have already set in motion the liberation of al-Masjid al-Aqṣā. It is likely that when we meet them in the Hereafter, we will say: "You have no idea what your sacrifice triggered. You changed the world." This is the essence and flowing benefits found in *ṣadaqah jāriyah* (continuous charity). The Prophet ﷺ taught us that even after death, the believer can continue earning rewards through the good they initiated via the following acts: 1) shared knowledge, 2) a child raised in righteousness, 3) a copy of the Qur'an passed down, 4) a built *masjid*, 5) a deep and nourishing well, or 6) a charity given sincerely while alive and capable.[262] Imam al-Mundhirī ﷺ noted that while a person's actions cease at death, their rewards continue if the impact remains.[263] This is because Allah, in His perfect justice, never lets even a trace of good go unrewarded. And sometimes, these deeds result in someone raising their hands in *du'ā'* for you, even if they never knew your name. Many of us are reconnected to Allah and the religion of Islam today because of the pain we witnessed in Gaza. It is very possible that our guidance and return to the straight path is their act of *ṣadaqah jāriyah*.

The physical world and the metaphysical plane of the Barzakh are not disconnected. They are woven together with divine threads. Because of this, *du'ā'* flows across these realms. And even if the signal is faint, the impact is nevertheless real. Your prayer might reach a soul in the grave, easing their burden or raising their rank. Al-'Abbās ibn Ya'qūb ﷺ narrated that a pious man saw his father in a dream. The father asked, "My son, why

262 *Sunan Ibn Mājah*, 242.

263 *'Aun al-Ma'bood*, 8:63

have you stopped sending gifts?" The son replied, "Do the dead really feel them?" The father said: "O my son, were it not for the living, the dead would fade away."[264] This powerful truth is further reflected in a statement from Sufyān ibn 'Uyaynah ﵀, who remarked:

اَلْمَوْتَى أَحْوَجُ إِلَى الدُّعَاءِ مِنَ الأَحْيَاءِ إِلَى الطَّعَامِ

"The dead are in greater need of du'ā' than the living are in need of food."[265]

Just as we increase our *du'ā'* in Ramadan, perhaps the souls in the graves feel the dryness of our absence. Our *du'ā'* can be a shield, a light, and an embodiment of mercy that soothes people who have left this world. There is a story of a man whose brother died which further underscores this theme. This man later saw his deceased brother in a dream and asked what happened at the moment of burial. The brother said: "A being approached me with a fire in its hand. Had it not been for one of your *du'ā's*, I would have been engulfed by it."[266] 'Amr ibn Jarīr ﵀ said that when a person prays for a deceased believer, an Angel delivers their *du'ā'* to their grave, saying:

يَا صَاحِبَ الْقَبْرِ الْغَرِيبِ هَدِيَّةٌ مِنْ أَخٍ عَلَيْكَ شَفِيقٍ

"O occupant of this lonely grave, here is a gift from a loving brother."[267]

264 Ibn Rajab al-Ḥanbalī, *Ahwāl al-Qubūr*, 134.

265 Ibn Rajab al-Ḥanbalī, *Ahwāl al-Qubūr*, 134.

266 Ibn al-Qayyim, *Kitāb al-Rūḥ*, vol. 1, 273.

267 Ibn al-Qayyim, *Kitāb al-Rūḥ*, vol. 1, 273.

Furthermore, it is narrated that one of the eminent members of the *salaf* (pious predecessors) saw a deceased friend in a dream. He asked: "Does the *du'ā'* of the living reach you?" The reply from the deceased person was the following: "By Allah, it arrives like a glowing light, and we decorate our graves with it."[268] So the next time you raise your hands in prayer, be mindful of this fact: your *du'ā'* might relieve someone's suffering in the grave, and might elevate their status in Jannah.

When a believer makes *du'ā'* for someone who has passed away—especially one enduring punishment in their grave—Allah may out of His mercy ease that person's suffering. And if the deceased is already in a state of comfort and reward, then the *du'ā'* becomes a means of further spiritual upliftment and elevation in rank. For instance, Bashār ibn Ghālib ﵀ said: "I once saw the devout worshipper Rābi'ah al-'Adawiyyah in a dream. I used to make recurrent *du'ā's* for her, so I asked, 'Do my prayers reach you?' She replied: 'O Bashar ibn al-Ghālib! Your *du'ā's* come to us like gifts that are carried on trays of light, wrapped in silk, and presented with honour.'" He asked, "How can that be?" She said, "This is the reality of the *du'ā'* of a living believer for the deceased. It is more precious than any gift you could have offered during our lifetime. What gift is more noble, more beautiful, and more lasting than a *du'ā'* that brings light into the darkness of the grave and expands its space with mercy?"[269]

---

268 Ibn al-Qayyim, *Kitāb al-Rūḥ*, vol. 1, 273.

269 Ibn al-Qayyim, *Kitāb al-Rūḥ*, vol. 1, 272.

As you look forward to the most sacred days and nights of the year, namely when your *du'ā's* carry weight like never before, strive to remember those souls who can no longer pray for themselves and wait in silence, hoping that someone among the living will remember them. Let your *du'ā'* be their light, ease, and joy in the unseen world.

"...so I may do good in what I left behind." Never! It is only a [useless] appeal they make. And there is a barrier [the Barzakh] behind them until the Day they are resurrected.

***AL-MU'MINŪN*, 23:100**

27

Laylat al-Qadr in the heavens and the graves

According to Islamic tradition, Laylat al-Qadr is the night when the Angels descend with peace, and the prayers of the believers ascend with power. Commonly translated as the Night of Decree or the Night of Power, Laylat al-Qadr is when the mercy of Allah envelops the Earth, and the unseen world responds to the call of His servants. Despite being only a single night, its virtue outweighs a thousand months; it thus equals a lifetime of worship condensed into a few hours. The souls in their graves, if given the chance, would trade anything for just one more moment to pray—even two brief *rak'ahs* (units)—on an ordinary day. Imagine, then, how much more they would long for another chance at worshipping their Creator on Laylat al-Qadr. Now, while they can no longer act, you still can perform virtuous deeds on their behalf. Many of your deceased loved ones also rely on your *du'ā'* to benefit them on such special days and events.

Laylat al-Qadr possesses a myriad of meanings and virtues that lie beyond the veil of this world. One of the meanings of its name is that the heavens are filled to their *qadr*, that is, their maximum capacity. On this special night, a wave of Angels traverse between the skies and the Earth, a number that is so intense that if their presence could be seen, it would outshine the Sun itself. They visit homes and *masjids* by carrying reports, registering deeds, recording names, and spreading the peace—inducing word of *salām* (greeting) until the break of dawn. If we could hear the mention of our names among the scrolls of the forgiven, we would desperately long to be counted among them. Yaḥyā ibn Mu'ādh ﵀ said: "O heedless one! O ignorant one! If you could hear the scratching of the pens in al-Lawḥ al-Maḥfūẓ (the Preserved Tablet), recording your name each time you remembered your Lord, you would die out of longing to meet Him."[270] May Allah allow us to see our names written in light, and to meet Him while He is pleased with us.

270 Abū Nu'aym al-Iṣbahānī, *Ḥilyah al-Awliyā' wa Ṭabaqāt al-Aṣfiyā'*, vol. 10, 56.

The righteous of the past centuries prayed and wept in this sacred night. And even after they passed away, they continued to observe Laylat al-Qadr from their graves, with their virtuous deeds still growing. Imam Ibn al-Jawzī ﵀ said, "By Allah, if the people of the graves were allowed one wish, they would wish for just one more day of Ramadan."[271] If that is their longing for an ordinary day in this blessed month, one could only imagine their eagerness for an opportunity to pray during the last ten nights.

There are some indications from the Shariah that the dead believers are aware of the arrival of special days and nights in the year, including Laylat al-Qadr. For instance, the Qur'an states that the people of the Barzakh experience time:

ٱلنَّارُ يُعْرَضُونَ عَلَيْهَا غُدُوًّا وَعَشِيًّا ۖ

"They are exposed to the Fire [in their graves] morning and evening."[272]

Furthermore, the Prophet ﷺ said that every soul is shown its place in Jannah or Jahannam each morning and evening. Thus, the deceased are not disconnected from the units of time and its movement. They hear of the world through the newly departed, and their deeds are presented to them. They also ask about the ones they loved. And many scholars affirm that the souls of the believers gather every Jumuʿah, just as the living

271 Ibn al-Jawzī, *al-Tabṣirah*, vol. 2, 78.

272 *Ghāfir*, 40:46.

On Laylat al-Qadr, a wave of Angels traverse between the skies and the Earth. They visit homes and *masjids* by carrying reports, registering deeds, recording names, and spreading the peace–inducing word of *salām* (greeting) until the break of dawn.

gather in the *masjid*.[273] This special and blessed day is a time of reunion, remembrance, and mercy. In his book *Kitāb al-Rūḥ*, Ibn al-Qayyim ﵀ strongly speaks of this connection. One chapter of his work is even titled, "What Do the Birds Utter on the Day of Jumuʿah?"

There is a narration which states that Muṭarrif ﵀ would visit the graveyard every Friday morning. One day, as he sat at the gate, he dozed off. In his dream, he saw the souls sitting atop their graves calling, "O Muṭarrif, the one who visits us every Jumʿuah!" He then saw birds flying above, chirping joyfully. He asked, "What are they saying?" The souls responded, "They are proclaiming: '*Salām* (peace) [to you] on a blessed day.'"[274] If that is the blessing of Jumʿuah, one could only imagine the blessings and metaphysical beauties that emerge on Laylat al-Qadr, which is when the heavens echo with *salām* until the morning. One could, for instance, consider the following verse regarding this special night:

سَلَامٌ هِيَ حَتَّىٰ مَطْلَعِ الْفَجْرِ

"It is all peace [on that night] until the break of dawn."[275]

Regarding this verse, Imam al-Ḍaḥḥāk ﵀ said: "On this night, Allah decrees nothing except peace. Even the stars are not allowed to shoot against the devils until dawn."[276]

---

273 al-Ḥasan al-Zuhayrī, *Sharḥ Uṣūl I'tiqād Ahl al-Sunnah*, vol. 57, 5.

274 Ibn ʿAsākir, *Tārīkh Madīnah Dimashq*, vol. 68, p. 322.

275 *al-Qadr*, 97:5.

276 Musāʿid bin Sulaymān, *Mawsūʿah al-Tafsīr al-Ma'thūr*, vol. 23, 430.

Every realm experiences a moment of stillness and a pause from evil. Even the dreams that are seen on this night are protected from the whispers or the plots of the devils. ʿAbdullāh ibn ʿAbbās said that the dream of Yūsuf—where he saw the Sun, the Moon, and the stars prostrate to him—occurred on Laylat al-Qadr.[277] Thus, even the people of the graves and those already in Jannah or its mirror opposite realm are affected. Those who have a window to their final destination feel its manifest effects. Imam Ibn al-Jawzī also said: "One reason for why it is called Laylat al-Qadr is that those who were previously seen as having no worth can now obtain such a standing by observing it and become people of *qadr* (divine value)."[278] That one night might change how Allah views us entirely, pulling us away from the scrolls of the condemned to the ranks of the righteous.

Everything that a person does on this night holds immense value, especially their *duʿā'*. The value that Laylat al-Qadr holds for us is commensurate to what the night of al-Isrā' wa al-Miʿrāj meant for the Prophet ﷺ. Ibn Taymiyyah beautifully draws this connection, stating: "The night of al-Isrā' is superior for the Prophet because of what he witnessed and received. Laylat al-Qadr is superior for the Ummah because of what they receive."[279] The Prophet ﷺ was taken through the realms of the Barzakh, meeting the Prophets in al-Aqṣā, conversing with the Angels, and even speaking with Allah Himself.

---

277 Makkī ibn Abī Ṭālib, *al-Hidāyah ilā Bulūgh al-Nihāyah*, vol. 5, 3501.

278 Ibn al-Jawzī, *al-Tabṣirah*, vol. 2, 92.

279 Cited in Ibn ʿUthaymīn, *Fatāwā Nūr ʿalā al-Darb*, Vol. 11, 2.

On Laylat al-Qadr,
if we could hear
the mention of
our names among
the scrolls of the
forgiven, we would
desperately long
to be counted
among them.

That was his night of divine access. Laylat al-Qadr, on the other hand, is our night of access. This is the night where our *du'ā's* rise, our deeds are magnified, and we are surrounded by Angels. Just as the Prophet ﷺ interceded for those he loved on the night of al-Isrā', we intercede for our loved ones—both living and deceased—on Laylat al-Qadr.

Recall the story of that father in the grave who told his son, "Do not stop sending your gifts to us." More specifically, he said, "O my son, ask Allah to grant us His pardon and His forgiveness."[280] On the night of Laylat al-Qadr, the Muslims supplicate to Allah with the following *du'ā'*, which is related from the Prophet ﷺ himself:

اللَّهُمَّ إِنَّكَ عَفُوٌّ تُحِبُّ الْعَفْوَ فَاعْفُ عَنَّا

"O Allah, You are the Pardoner, You love to pardon, so pardon us."[281]

When making this collective supplication, it is imperative to have the deceased Muslims in mind when reciting that final "us" portion of the *du'ā'*. This world is a stage that is brimming with physical and metaphysical realities. We perform virtuous deeds before the unseen, striving for rewards we cannot yet see. Undoubtedly, Laylat al-Qadr is the grandest night of that performance. How blessed is the one who lives to witness it, and how truly blessed is the one who one day sees, in the Barzakh, everything it did for them and for those they loved!

280 Ibn Rajab al-Ḥanbalī, *Ahwāl al-Qubūr*, 134.

281 *Sunan Ibn Mājah*, 3850.

28

Your *tahajjud* could get you into Jannah

Tahajjud (voluntary night prayers after sleep) is the key to your spiritual success. When the world sleeps, you can and should rise quietly and sincerely, such that your soul is drawn to a stillness where only Allah hears you. That way, the night becomes your confidant, and your prayer is transformed into a deep secret between your heart and the Most Merciful. Such an intimate prayer in the depths of the night is hidden from the eyes of people, but known fully to the Lord of the unseen.

Ḥabībah al-ʿAdawiyyah would climb to her rooftop after the ʿIshāʾ prayer and call out:

إِلٰهِي غَارَتِ النُّجُومُ وَنَامَتِ الْعُيُونُ وَغَلَّقَتِ الْمُلُوكُ أَبْوَابَهَا وَبَابُكَ
مَفْتُوحٌ وَخَلَا كُلُّ حَبِيبٍ بِحَبِيبِهِ وَهَذَا مَقَامِي بَيْنَ يَدَيْكَ

"O Allah, the stars have set, the eyes have closed, and the kings have locked their doors. But Your door remains open. Every lover is alone with their beloved, and here I am, standing before You."[282]

Such is the soul that rises while others sleep, whereby it ascends in closeness even while the body remains still. Manṣūr ibn al-Muʿtamir prayed every night on his rooftop with such an impressive degree of consistency that after his death a young boy asked his mother, "Where did that pole on Mansūr's rooftop go?" She replied, "O my son, that was not a pole. Rather it was Manṣūr standing in prayer."[283] A child noticed his absence, but something far greater than that is the fact that Allah noticed his presence. Maybe you tasted that sweetness yourself last night. Maybe you stood in prayer, whispered a sincere *duʿā'*, or shed a tear that watered your grave's garden. And then after Fajr you slept deeply with the kind of rest that only comes from a night spent in striving for Allah's pleasure.

282 Ibn al-Jawzī, *Ṣifah al-Ṣafwah*, vol. 2, 246.

283 al-Dhahabī, *Siyar Aʿlām al-Nubalā'*, vol. 5, 406.

The Prophet ﷺ described the first night in the grave for the righteous as the sleep of a newlywed, such that it is deep and peaceful, and awakened only by the most beloved of things. You might wake to see the very garden that your prayer built. Or perhaps, unknown to you, someone else's suffering in the grave ended because you remembered them in your *du'ā'*.

Qiyām al-layl (voluntary night prayers) is the secret joy of the believers, whereby it fills their hearts with light before Paradise fills their eyes. Abū Sulaymān al-Dārānī ﷺ once poignantly said:

لَوْلَا اللَّيْلُ مَا أَحْبَبْتُ الْبَقَاءَ فِي الدُّنْيَا

"If it were not for the night prayer, I would have no desire to stay in this world."[284]

The tears you shed out of awe and fear of Allah are more than emotion; they are also a means of elevation. Abū Bakr ibn Abī Maryam ﷺ saw a man in a dream after death and asked him, "What did you find to be the greatest of your deeds?" He answered, "My tears that fell due to the fear of Allah."[285] Thus, even your weeping is not wasted; it becomes the spiritual fuel of your ascent. In another vision, Allah said of Mi'sār ibn Kidām ﷺ, a servant known for night worship: "Glad tidings to My servant, who longed for Me in the night.

284 Abū Nu'aym al-Isbahānī, *Ḥilyah al-Awliyā' wa Ṭabaqāt al-Aṣfiyā'*, vol. 9, 275.
285 Ibn al-Qayyim, *Kitāb al-Rūḥ*, vol. 1, 71.

Let him now behold My face and choose from the palaces of Paradise whatever he desires."[286] Voluntary prayer is an extremely virtuous act in Islam, and it falls under the domain of the following Qur'anic verse:

وَاسْجُدْ وَاقْتَرِبْ

"Rather, [continue to] prostrate and draw near [to Allah]."[287]

This verse constitutes a call to closeness that no heart should ignore. Laylat al-Qadr may be the pinnacle of nearness, but every night in the last third portion offers a window to intimacy with your Lord. In the Barzakh, those who gave life to the night with prayer will be brought in closer proximity to Allah. Qabīṣah ibn 'Uqbah ﷺ saw Sufyān al-Thawrī ﷺ in a dream and asked him, "What did Allah do for you?" He replied:

نَظَرْتُ إِلَى رَبِّي عِيَانًا فَقَالَ لِي ... هَنِيئًا رِضَايَا عَنْكَ يَا ابْنَ سَعِيدِ
لَقَدْ كُنْتَ قَوَّامًا إِذَا اللَّيْلُ قَدْ دَجَا ... بِعَبْرَةِ مَحْزُونٍ وَقَلْبِ عَمِيدِ
فَدُونَكَ فَاخْتَرْ أَيَّ قَصْرٍ تُرِيدُهُ ... وَزُرْنِي فَإِنِّي مِنْكَ غَيْرُ بَعِيدِ

"I beheld my Lord, clear and manifest, and He said to me:
'Take joy in My favour upon you, O blessed one, O son of Saʿīd!
You were among those who rose by night in devotion,
With a heart weighed in grief and eyes brimming with tears.
Now choose whatever mansion your soul desires is yours,
And come to Me, for I am ever near and never far.'"[288]

---

286 Ibn al-Qayyim, *Kitāb al-Rūḥ*, vol. 1, 79.

287 *al-'Alaq*, 96:18.

288 Abū Nu'aym al-Iṣbahānī, *Ḥilyah al-Awliyā' wa Ṭabaqāt al-Aṣfiyā'*, vol. 7, p. 74.

Tahajjud is not just a habit or custom; in reality, it is a hidden treasure and a gift between you and Allah. It draws no applause from the people or the public sphere, but from it comes endless rewards from the One Who knows all secrets. ʿAbdullāh ibn Masʿūd ﷺ said:

فَضْلُ صَلاَةِ اللَّيْلِ عَلَى صَلاَةِ النَّهَارِ كَفَضْلِ صَدَقَةِ السِّرِّ عَلَى صَدَقَةِ العَلاَنِيَةِ

"The superiority of night prayer over day prayer is like that of secret charity over public charity."[289]

Ibn Rajab ﷺ explained Ibn Masʿūd's statement by observing that the night prayer is a private affair, and therefore, more sincere and heartfelt.[290] While others worry about the secrets that may confront them in their graves, the person observing *qiyām al-layl* is planting a secret garden with Allah. One of the companions of Rābiʿah al-ʿAdawiyyah ﷺ saw her in a dream and made the following request, "Guide me to something that will bring me closer to Allah." She said, "Remember Him often because soon you will rejoice in your grave because of it."[291] Another righteous soul saw the ascetic Abū Bakr al-Shiblī ﷺ in a dream after his death, whereby the latter was dressed in fine clothes, firm in his place. When asked who his closest companions were, he replied: "Those who remembered Allah the most, who honoured His rights, and sought only His pleasure."[292]

289 Ibn Rajab, *Laṭāʾif al-Maʿārif*, p. 76.

290 Ibn Rajab, *Laṭāʾif al-Maʿārif*, p. 76.

291 Ibn al-Qayyim, *Kitāb al-Rūḥ*, vol. 1, 68.

292 Ibn al-Qayyim, *Kitāb al-Rūḥ*, vol. 1, 82.

This very theme is underscored in the following verse:

تَتَجَافَىٰ جُنُوبُهُمْ عَنِ ٱلْمَضَاجِعِ يَدْعُونَ رَبَّهُمْ خَوْفًا وَطَمَعًا وَمِمَّا رَزَقْنَٰهُمْ يُنفِقُونَ

"They abandon their beds, invoking their Lord with hope and fear, and donate from what We have provided for them."[293]

To encourage His servants to observe the nights in prayer, Allah states the following in the subsequent verse of the same chapter:

فَلَا تَعْلَمُ نَفْسٌ مَّآ أُخْفِيَ لَهُم مِّن قُرَّةِ أَعْيُنٍ جَزَآءًۢ بِمَا كَانُوا يَعْمَلُونَ

"No soul can imagine what delights are kept in store for them as a reward for what they used to do."[294]

When Allah unveils to you what He had stored for you—just for those nights you rose while others rested—will you not wish you had risen even more?

---

293 *al-Sajdah*, 32:16.

294 *al-Sajdah*, 32:17.

29

Everyone will have regrets

Every soul will experience some degree of regret when it enters the grave; no person can escape such a reality. In the Barzakh, every person will express the words, "If only I did such and such..." etched into their memory. The Prophet ﷺ said, as narrated by Abū Hurayrah ﷺ in the *Sunan* of al-Tirmidhī ﷺ:

مَا مِنْ أَحَدٍ يَمُوتُ إِلاَّ نَدِمَ

"No one dies except that they will experience regret."

The Companions asked, "What will they regret, O Messenger of Allah?" The Prophet ﷺ replied by stating:

إِنْ كَانَ مُحْسِنًا نَدِمَ أَنْ لاَ يَكُونَ ازْدَادَ وَإِنْ كَانَ مُسِيئًا نَدِمَ أَنْ لاَ يَكُونَ نَزَعَ

"If he was righteous, he will regret not having done more. And if he was sinful, he will regret not having stopped."[295]

Upon entering the grave, the believer may first wish to return—even for just a moment—to inform their loved ones the good news of their salvation. But soon, that desire gives way to something greater: longing for the reward and reunion that awaits in the next world. As for the disbeliever, they plead not to be brought forward to the Day of Judgment; this is not because they hope for this world again, but out of the fear and terror for their imminent doom. It is common for people to experience moments when they think, "I am not going to succeed." Some may even whisper to themselves, "I wish I was never born." Even the righteous predecessors had moments of introspection like these thoughts. 'Aṭā' al-Sulamī ؒ was known for his constant grief. His students once overheard him say to himself: "I wish 'Aṭā's mother never gave birth to him." He would often pray with the following *du'ā'* (supplication): "O Allah, have mercy on my loneliness in this world, have mercy on me at the moment of my death, and have mercy on my standing before You."[296] Later, Ṣāliḥ ibn Bishr ؒ saw him in a dream and said, "You were so sorrowful in the world!

295 *Sunan al-Tirmidhī*, 2403.

296 Abū Nu'aym al-Iṣbahānī, *Ḥilyah al-Awliyā' wa Ṭabaqāt al-Aṣfiyā'*, vol. 6, 216.

May Allah have mercy on you." 'Aṭā' responded by stating, "That sorrow has now turned into everlasting joy and delight." When asked about his rank, he said,

مَعَ الَّذِينَ أَنْعَمَ اللَّهُ عَلَيْهِمْ مِنَ النَّبِيِّينَ وَالصِّدِّيقِينَ وَالشُّهَدَاءِ وَالصَّالِحِينَ، وَحَسُنَ أُولَئِكَ رَفِيقًا

"I am 'with those whom Allah has favoured among the Prophets, the truthful, the martyrs, and the righteous. And what a blessed company that is!'[297]**"**[298]

Even when one ascends among the elite in the Barzakh, regret remains a reality. The feeling that one could have performed better to improve their rank never fully disappears. Ibn al-Qayyim ﵀ recounts seeing his teacher Ibn Taymiyyah ﵀ in a dream, where the latter was in a station so lofty that it surpassed many of the greats. Ibn Taymiyyah gestured toward his high rank and then said, "You almost reached us, but you stopped just short, and are now at the rank of Ibn Khuzaymah."[299] It was a gentle push and reminder for his pupil to continue striving and ascending through their righteous deeds.

Now consider the people of Gaza, who have endured unimaginable suffering during the last 1.5 years. You might wonder if some of them ever wished they were never born in the first place. But through the lens of the prophetic ethos, you begin to understand that they would in fact do it all over again and undergo whatever they were forced to experience.

---

297 *al-Nisā'*, 4:69.

298 Ibn al-Qayyim, *Kitāb al-Rūḥ*, vol. 1, 24.

299 Ibn Rajab, *Dhayl Ṭabaqāt al-Ḥanābilah*, vol. 5, 176.

Every soul will wish they had exerted greater efforts, prayed more, repented earlier, and strived harder. Before you lies a golden opportunity to change your story, to erase your regret, and to build your reward.

The Prophet ﷺ said, "No one who enters Paradise will wish to return to this world for anything, with the exception of the martyr. For he would wish to return and be killed ten times over for the honour he sees from Allah."[300] Even those who were mutilated, like the father of Jābir ibn ʿAbdullāh ﷺ at Uḥud, wished to come back. This desire to return is not for worldly pleasures, but due to the eternal beauty their souls now witness for the sacrifices they made in this world.

Every deceased person wishes to return to the world, but their reasons differ. The disbeliever aspires to return to the temporal world so they may believe. The sinner wishes to return so they may repent. And finally, the righteous asks their Lord to come back so they may expand their register of good deeds. Every soul will wish they had exerted greater efforts, prayed more, repented earlier, and strived harder. Allah says:

حَتَّىٰٓ إِذَا جَآءَ أَحَدَهُمُ ٱلْمَوْتُ قَالَ رَبِّ ٱرْجِعُونِ، لَعَلِّيٓ أَعْمَلُ صَٰلِحًا فِيمَا تَرَكْتُ،
كَلَّآ إِنَّهَا كَلِمَةٌ هُوَ قَآئِلُهَا، وَمِن وَرَآئِهِم بَرْزَخٌ إِلَىٰ يَوْمِ يُبْعَثُونَ

"When death approaches any of them, they cry, 'My Lord! Let me go back, so I may do good in what I left behind.' Never! It is only a [useless] appeal they make. And there is a barrier [i.e. the Barzakh] behind them until the Day they are resurrected."[301]

300 *Ṣaḥīḥ al-Bukhārī*, 2817.

301 *al-Mu'minūn*, 23:99-100.

Yet, one should note that no one in the Barzakh regrets the missed opportunity of procuring a source of employment, a house, a degree, or a marriage in this temporary world. No one laments stating, "If only I acquired and earned that work opportunity," or by remarking to themselves, "If only I had obtained more money, more status, more likes, and more recognition." Instead, they only regret the minutes that were not spent in remembrance of the divine, the prayers they performed without tranquillity, and the sins not erased with repentance. They also pity themselves for delaying the performance of good deeds until it was too late.

If you are still alive in this world, then you have been given something that every deceased person longs for: a chance. Before you lies a golden opportunity to change your story, to erase your regret, and to build your reward. And when the end comes, we pray it finds us in a state where the only thing we say is not "if only", but instead the declaration, "*Alḥamdulillāh* (all praise to Allah) that I returned to You, O Allah, with something to show."

Having hope in Allah

At the moment of death, the most powerful piece of advice that the Prophet ﷺ taught is observing the beautiful mental state of *ḥusn al-ẓann* (assuming well) of our Creator ﷻ.[302] When everything else becomes obsolete, the deeds have ended, and the soul prepares to depart, what Allah ﷻ seeks from you is observing and having firm trust in His infinite mercy. Abu Yaʿqūb al-Qārī رحمه الله saw a striking man in a dream who was tall

302 al-Tabrīzī, *Mishkāh al-Maṣābīḥ*, 81.

and brown-skinned, followed by a large crowd. He asked who it was, and they told him: "That is Uways al-Qarnī, the noble Successor from Yemen." So he followed him, issuing to him the following plea, "Give me advice, may Allah have mercy on you." Uways ﵀ did not provide any response. But Abu Ya'qūb al-Qārī ﵀ repeated himself, saying with greater urgency: "Please guide me." Almost immediately thereafter, Uways ﵀ turned around and said, "Pursue Allah's mercy while your heart is full of love for Him. Be cautious of His punishment, especially when you fall into sin. And no matter what your state is, never stop having hope in Him."[303]

A man dreamt of Mālik ibn Dīnār ﵀ after his death. Interestingly, Mālik was the same person who returned to the path of Allah through a vision of his daughter. In the dream, the man asked Mālik, "What did you bring to Allah?" Mālik replied: "I came burdened with sins, but I met Allah with unwavering hope, and it was that hope which erased them all."[304] 'Abdullāh ibn 'Umar, the son of the great Umayyad Caliph 'Umar ibn 'Abd al-'Azīz ﵀, once related that he saw his father in a dream; the latter was in a garden, offering him apples. He asked, "What deed meant the most to you?" His father answered: "*Istighfār* (seeking forgiveness of Allah). Allah is generous with the one who asks with confidence and trust."[305] Another man saw al-Ḥasan ibn Ṣāliḥ ﵀ in a dream and told him, "I waited so long to hear from you." Al-Ḥasan simply

303 Ibn Abī al-Dunyā, *al-Manāmāt*, 51.

304 Ibn Abī al-Dunyā, *al-Manāmāt*, 33.

305 Ibn Abī al-Dunyā, *al-Manāmāt*, 28.

said: "Rejoice. Nothing benefits a believer more than expecting the best from Allah."[306] When 'Abd al-'Azīz ibn Sulaymān ﵀ passed away, several people saw him in a dream, where he was dressed in lush green garments and adorned with a crown of pearls. They asked him, "How was your death? How is your life now?" He replied: "The pain of death? Do not ask about that. But it was Allah's mercy that covered my faults, and without that mercy, I would have been lost."[307]

Throughout this work's chapters, readers have become well-acquainted with the terrifying accounts of the grave, such as the questioning, the constriction, and the darkness. However, it is important to note that it is not one's deeds that ensure one's salvation. Rather, it is always Allah and His mercy. You may wonder now and ask yourself: what will happen to me when my soul is taken? And what is the state and condition of those who have already passed? But just look at what Allah has given us. He provides us the month of repentance, namely Ramadan, which confers a golden opportunity to return to Him. He provides us all with the precious pearl of Laylat al-Qadr, a single night that is worth a lifetime. He would not offer us so many chances unless He wanted to forgive us. All we have to do is to sincerely desire His love and forgiveness and perform acts of virtue.

306 Ibn Abī al-Dunyā, *al-Manāmāt*, 42.

307 Ibn Abī al-Dunyā, *al-Manāmāt*, 45.

As this journey ends, we must remember that Allah ﷻ never turns away from the one who sincerely seeks Him. The Ramadan of this year may be over, but our connection to Allah does not have to end. For He is always near as long as the servant's heart continues to pursue His love and guidance. With this point in mind, it is fitting to close this work with a final *du'ā'* that is based on the words of the Prophet ﷺ: "O Allah, I ask You for a life of peace after death, the joy of seeing Your Face, and the longing to meet You not because of a harmful adversity, or fear of a misleading trial."[308]

May Allah ﷻ protect us and forgive us. May He accept from us, lift the burden of our brothers and sisters in Gaza and beyond, and reunite us with them in the pleasant planes of the Barzakh and the eternal gardens of Jannah al-Firdaws in the Hereafter. *Āmīn*.

308 *Sunan al-Nasā'ī*, 1305.

Allah never turns away from the one who sincerely seeks Him. He is always near as long as the servant's heart continues to pursue His love and guidance. May Allah grant us a pleasant experience in the Barzakh and an eternal home in Paradise. *Āmīn*.